PERSUASION

PERSUASION

THE ART OF GETTING WHAT YOU WANT

Dave Lakhani

WILEY

JOHN WILEY & SONS, INC.

Published by John Wiley & Sons, Inc., Hoboken, New Jersey.
Published simultaneously in Canada.

For general information on our other products and services please contact our Customer Care Department within the U.S. at (800) 762-2974, outside the United States at (317) 572-3993 or fax (317) 572-4002.

Wiley also publishes its books in a variety of electronic formats. Some content that appears in print may not be available in electronic books. For more information about Wiley products, visit our web site at www.wiley.com.

Library of Congress Cataloging-in-Publication Data:
Lakhani, Dave, 1965–
    Persuasion : the art of getting what you want / Dave Lakhani.
      p.   cm.
    Includes bibliographical references and index.
    ISBN-13 978-0-471-73044-6 (hardcover)
    ISBN-10 0-471-73044-0 (hardcover)
  1. Persuasion (Psychology)   I. Title.
    BF637.P4L32 2005
    303.3'42—dc22

                                        2005005163

Printed in the United States of America.

10 9 8 7 6 5 4 3 2 1

This book is dedicated with love to the four most important women in my life:

My grandmother—Edith Ramsey McManus
My mother—Joanna Lakhani-Willard
My wife—Stephanie Lakhani
My daughter—Austria Raine Lakhani

Also to my brothers:
Bill Willard Jr.
Mike Willard

And my closest friends:
Thomas "Ted" Goodier
Bill Braseth
Rodney Schlienz
Steve Watts
Ronald "John" Stukey

CONTENTS

FOREWORD

E veryone wants it their way.

You have been trying to persuade people since you were a baby. Crying, smiling, banging your hands on the table. Primitive, to be sure—but effective.

Remember the aisle of the grocery store with your mom? Begging for that candy bar? *That* was persuasion.

Remember high school dating? *That* was persuasion.

But it seems that after you got your business cards printed, some of the tenacity associated with your persuasion skills has been missing.

Fear not. This book has the persuasion answers you're looking for, whether it's sales, service, internal communications, friends, or family.

Getting others to see your perspective, agree with your ideas, do what you want them to do, or just simply agree with you is a skill and a science. And in this book you will learn that skill.

Persuasion is not just a selling skill. Persuasion is a life skill.

Throughout this book you will gently be prodded to change your ways of thinking and interacting with others with regard to everything from what you wear to what your body says. You'll be asked to do things, take actions. And you will do them. What better way to learn persuasion than to see yourself being persuaded, taking action as a result of it, and loving it?

The key to persuasion is to let the other person feel great after he or she has decided to see it or do it your way. In order to accomplish this, there has to be an understanding of how to best persuade.

The easiest persuasion answer is given inside this book: Get others to persuade themselves. This is done by asking questions.

Persuasion is an outcome. The secret of persuasion's happy outcome is two words: manipulation free. Manipulated persuasion is short lived. True persuasion exists when it lasts beyond the moment.

Persuasion is an art.
Persuasion is a science.
Persuasion is compromise.
Persuasion is excellent communication skills.
Persuasion is asking questions that clarify the situation.
Persuasion is getting the other guy to convince himself.
Persuasion is reading this book—and putting the principles
    into action.
Persuasion is an outcome.
Persuasion is a victory.

"I did it my way!" is *not* the way that song should have ended. If Frank or Elvis were masters of persuasion, they would have sung:

"I did it my way, and everyone agreed with me!"

Why not learn more ways of getting others to see it your way?

If you agree with me so far, just turn to the next page. . . .

Jeffrey Gitomer

PREFACE

Leave me penniless and naked in any town in America and by the end of the day I'll have clothes, food, lodging, a way of earning an income, a following, and enough money in my pocket to start again. Why? Because I know exactly how to persuade people to do what I need them to do for both of us to achieve our goals.

—Dave Lakhani

Virtually every element of human interaction involves some level of persuasion, but particularly sales, negotiation, copywriting, advertising, and media relations. Many scholars, philosophers, and scientists have explored the process, yet few get it right consistently. They dismiss the fundamental survival requirement of persuasion. They've analyzed it as a process that can be used if necessary, but don't understand that persuasion isn't a tool we use optionally; it is one we are required to use in order to survive. The essence of life itself is persuasion, how well we persuade ourselves, how well we persuade those around us, and how we are ourselves persuaded by those who persuade us.

This book began with my first study of the persuasion process more than 24 years ago and has continued to develop since then. Throughout the book I demonstrate how persuasion works in person, in the media, in advertising, and in sales. I also demonstrate specific steps you can use to develop your persuasiveness, charisma, and ability to influence others in order to get what you want. I show you how to incorporate the process into your everyday life so that you are able to influence and persuade effectively and unconsciously. It will become as natural as speaking or walking.

This book is different than any book you've read about persuasion, sales, or negotiation. The differences are profound in several ways. First, it is not my intention to scientifically break down exactly why people make the decisions they do and the psychological methodologies for creating change in people. What I do is demonstrate, in the first section, the difference between persuasion and manipulation. The second portion of the book focuses on the key areas and elements involved in rapid persuasion.

My only real interest (and I believe yours, as well) is to persuade . . . fast. Therefore, I believe the best way to do that is to give you an overview of the elements and a description of why it is important to you and then dig right into how to make it work for you. I'm not going to bother you with a lot of arcane references, only those most appropriate to your success.

Finally, in the third section of the book I demonstrate the Persuasion Equation™, which ties it all together and gives you a practical format for quickly persuading anyone. This portion of the book has been described as dangerous and genius alike by those who have attended my seminars and speaking engagements. Quite simply, the Persuasion Equation demonstrates how to apply every technique you learn in the second section of the book in order to move people to your position or to take the action you want them to take. People think it is genius because of the simplicity of the program and dangerous because it is also the very same process you use to manipulate another person. Your intention will ultimately determine whether you've persuaded or manipulated, and if you decided to manipulate someone, whether it was appropriate. Ultimately only you can make that judgment call.

Interestingly, whether you are persuading as a profession or just need to get a date with the perfect man or woman, the processes that I teach you will work perfectly. I have broken down a few areas that I think you'll find very valuable. For example, I have included sections on writing, negotiation, advertising, and selling. Those sections will help you understand how to use the process in very specific professional persuasion situations and to improve your ability in each.

I began studying persuasion for a rather unusual reason. I was raised by a brilliant single mother who wanted the very best for my brothers and me. Mom was literate, creative, well spoken, motivated, and focused on a better life for all of us . . . so she decided to raise us in a religious cult.

Before I explain why that led to my study of persuasion, let me tell you a bit about this unique cult because it really was the impetus for my very thorough study of persuasion, manipulation, and influence.

When I say "religious cult," I'm not talking about a mainstream fundamental Christian church, quite the opposite in fact.

xvi   PREFACE

Although there was a fundamental belief in God as Savior, that is
where the similarity to traditional religion ended. They believed
that women had very little value in society beyond giving birth
and caring for their children, their home, and their husbands.
Education was strongly discouraged, boys were to be out of
school by the eighth grade at the latest, and many young women
were out of school by the sixth or seventh grade and "home
schooled" through the years required by the state. There was
also no television, no radio, no dancing, no dating outside the
church, and no divorce was allowed. Women could not cut their
hair, wear makeup, or wear any garment that pertained to a man
(pants in particular), and men were required to keep very short
haircuts, be clean-shaven, and be the primary breadwinner for
the family.

Church services were very strict, too: Tuesdays, Thursdays,
twice on Sunday, and often a Friday-night prayer meeting. Services were the fire and brimstone kind and they often lasted
longer than three hours. There was no talking, moving, or fid-
dling around in church, either. The deacons enforced that and
any young children who dared disobey (or even to be bored out
of their minds enough to fidget) were immediately taken to the
back of the church and punished if their parents didn't do it in a
timely manner. When it was time for punishment, there was no
sparing the rod or spoiling the child.

One of my younger brothers suffered terribly during those
years. He had what would now likely be diagnosed as attention
deficit disorder and what has since tested as a very high IQ. The
leaders of the church diagnosed him as "having the Devil in
him," and prescribed regular beatings to get the Devil out of
him. I often marveled at the power of the Devil in my brother,
because no amount of beating or other physical punishment

could dislodge it. (In truth, I hold both my brothers in highest regard and awe for their ability to endure and survive what surely would have ruined if not killed others, and for coming out of it well adjusted and successful.) Beating a child so severely and regularly that he often could barely walk would dislodge most devils.

You see, it was important to get the Devil out because the "Bible Believers," as the followers of the end-time prophet William Branham were called, knew that there was going to be a very literal rapture in the very near future and only those who were "Bible Believers" like them would be taken up in the rapture and given access to God's kingdom. Everyone else would suffer in tribulation on the earth until the resurrection when the dead would rise and then everything in the book of Revelation would occur literally and the largest majority of those left would be hastened to the lake of fire.

Sounds almost surreal, doesn't it? Even my condensed version of the story demonstrates obvious problems in logic. But what amazed me most, as I grew older, was the number of people that accepted this story I've just told you without question. Many of those people were well educated, and from well-adjusted homes, though not all. Day after day, year after year, those very same people willingly gave up much of what they earned to support a minister (to whom many of the rules didn't apply), and a church, all while spreading the good word and attracting even more people to the church and drawing them in systematically until they, too, were completely hooked.

I was involved in the church from the time I was 7 years old until I was 16 when I finally made a decision on my own that I'd have to leave the church if I intended to complete my education and if I wanted to stop bringing additional problems home to my family. In order to leave the church, I'd also have to leave home. So, shortly after my sixteenth birthday I made my intentions known to my mother and to the church and was summarily excommunicated with a prayer to God that He would turn my soul over to Satan for the destruction of my flesh that I might see the error of my ways, repent, and return to church (I have to laughingly admit, a few times through my life I've wondered if their prayer was working).

The very next day I moved away from home and retreated to the one place where I'd always found solace and a never-ending source of food for my question-filled brain . . . the library. At the library I began studying what exactly drew people to cults, specifically, how someone as bright and creative and wonderful as my mom could be convinced that everything she knew and held true was wrong and everything these new people said was right, and how I could persuade her that there was a better, smarter, and healthier way for all of us to live.

The story I have shared with you is a story not of persuasion, but rather one of manipulation. This is not a book about cults, although I discuss how to create a cult-like customer following. It is not about the negative sort of manipulation that does not create a lasting relationship, although I teach you precisely how to manipulate so you can understand how it occurs and defend yourself from it and ensure you are not guilty of it. In the beginning of the book I discuss manipulation, how it happens, and why it works . . . for a while. You'll see that many facets of effective persuasion are inherent in manipulation, but it is the subtle differences and outcomes that set the two clearly apart. Ultimately, manipulation always fails, but true persuasion lasts.

This is a book about persuasion and the art of using persuasion to get exactly what you want. In getting what you want, you'll also position yourself as an expert in helping others get what they want and that is the highest form of persuasion. What I found out over those ensuing years I share with you here because the strategy and tactics I learned for changing minds, for creating winning situations for all, for getting what I wanted will allow you to quickly and easily get everything you've ever wanted out of life.

The strategies I am about to share with you are not the strategies of the manipulative cultist, but the specific ethical patterns, processes, and tactics you can use to get more of what you want out of this life. By simply understanding the elements of persuasion that must be present for you to succeed, you succeed more often. True persuasion is based in truth, honesty, inquisitiveness, and the ability to tell a good story and to elicit the persuasion criteria of those you hope to persuade so you can meet their expectations easily. I also show you how manipulation happens and why manipulation is always bad and never works long term, and how to use the positive and very powerful tools of persuasion that instantly change minds and compel people to action to get exactly what you want out of life, just as I have.

By learning how to ethically persuade I have achieved every major goal I have ever set for myself by being able to quickly and efficiently persuade not only others but also myself. Along the way, I have helped many people whom I have persuaded reach one of their goals, too. I have consistently achieved an income that puts me in the top 3 to 5 percent of income earners in the United States. I have been able to get the best jobs, access to the best minds, and access to the very best people (like you) to learn with and support my efforts. I have done more in my 40-plus years than most people will do in a lifetime and, like you, I have so much more to do before it is over.

My mom did finally see the many thinking errors of the church and eventually left about three years after I left home, but the pull was so strong and the influence so high that on her deathbed she questioned whether she had made a big mistake by leaving the church.

After Mom's death in 1999, I began to ponder deeply what caused her to continue to question her decision even after she saw the error of the beliefs that kept her connected to the church for so long. The longer I thought about the issue the more I began to think about it in the context of business as well.

And that thought made me ask this question: "Shouldn't your customers wonder if they leave you if they just made the biggest mistake of their lives?" Throughout the pages of this book I demonstrate how you can create a cult-like following of customers who, even if they leave, will always wonder if they made the right decision. That concern, combined with your ethical ability to serve them better, will draw them back—or will keep most of them from ever leaving in the first place. Belief perseverance is a powerful concept we'll explore in much more detail later.

If you have ever dreamed that there is more to life than what you are getting right now, if you have ever wanted a raise, a better job, more sales, better deals, better "things," the perfect partner, or a better life, I am going to show you what insiders, the "born salespeople," and the true persuaders know. I am going to show you how to get exactly what you want whenever you want it. I also show you how to avoid the mistakes I made along the way to shorten your learning curve.

If you will allow me, over the next few pages I will personally teach you, groom you, coach you, and lead you through a new skill your parents didn't know they should teach you, isn't taught in any school, and often isn't discussed in polite company, but one that will serve you well for the rest of your life. I will demonstrate how you can master *Persuasion—The Art of Getting What You Want.*

ACKNOWLEDGMENTS

I t is impossible to write a book without a great deal of help from very willing and understanding people. This book is certainly no exception to this rule and I'd like to thank a few of those people here. If I missed you it wasn't intentional, and I do thank you.

My highest thanks go to several people but especially to Joe Vitale, an interesting man and an amazing author, for all he did to help this book come to life, and to Matt Holt, my editor at Wiley, who was so easy to work with and who helped me navigate this process so willingly. To Robert Greene, author of two of the most important books on persuasion ever written, *The 48 Laws of Power* (Penguin Putnam, 2001) and *The Art of Seduction* (Penguin Books, 2003), a very special thanks for spending several hours with me as he was in the midst of finishing his next book. I'd also like to thank Angela Dailey, psychologist and friend, for her valuable contribution, and to thank all of the other contributors who I interviewed to make this book great. Kathy McIntosh, thanks for helping me edit. Your contributions were invaluable.

To all of my clients and students, thanks for asking such great questions; you make thinking fun! Thanks to Steve Watts (an amazing persuader) for being a great friend and for helping me prove or disprove a lot of the ideas that you'll find in this book, and to all the great salespeople I've had a chance to work with, especially Todd Carlson, John Miller, Ryan Valentine, Nattalie Hoch, and Angela Karp. To all of the Below The Radar Wizards, thanks for all the encouragement. Thanks go to Jana Kemp, who listens as fast as I think and talk. Caitlin Stellflug, thanks for keeping the office running while I was writing.

My most important thanks go to everyone I've ever persuaded in any way. Thanks for the experience and the feedback. You truly made this book possible.

There are a number of people who have been ever supportive of all I've done in a very full and ever-changing life; their encouragement was invaluable during this process as well. Rod and Casey Schlienz, Bill and Sandra Braseth, Ted and Sherri Goodier, thanks for always being there. To Dr. John Stukey, who is, as I write this, serving our country honorably in Iraq, and whose support I've never had to think about because it was always there, thank you. Of course no acknowledgment would be complete without acknowledging the contribution of the Nurnberg DST team, "The Regan Years," and The Four Horsemen. Those ideals that we began building way back then will be very evident here.

In the Preface I describe a time in my life that was very confusing but led to over 20 years of research that have gone into this book. During that time, there were four people who I respected and trusted and who always helped me learn and see what was possible, and who supported me even when they disagreed. For that Shawn and Linda Lee, Kevin Lee, and Richard Dailey, thank you.

Finally, to my wife and daughter, who thought I'd gotten lost or trapped in my office, thanks for the snacks and the laughs, but most of all the understanding. You make all I do worthwhile. I love you.

Dave Lakhani

ABOUT THE AUTHOR

Dave Lakhani is the world's first Business Acceleration Strategist™ and President of Bold Approach, Inc., a Business Acceleration Strategy firm helping companies worldwide immediately increase their revenue through effective sales, marketing, and public relations.

Dave is considered one of the world's top experts on the application of persuasion and his talks are in high demand and heard by corporations and trade organizations of all sizes worldwide. His advice is regularly seen in *Selling Power* magazine, *Sales and Marketing Management*, the *Wall Street Journal*, *Investors Business Daily*, *INC.*, *Entrepreneur*, *The Today Show*, and hundreds of other media outlets. Dave is also the host of *Making Marketing Work*, a radio talk show focused on marketing strategy for growing businesses. Dave also authored *A Fighting Chance* (Prince Publishing, 1991), a section of the anthology *Ready, Aim, Hire* (Persysco,

1992), and the audio book *Making Marketing Work* (BA Books, 2004).

Dave has owned more than 10 successful businesses in the last 20 years and considers himself a serial entrepreneur and committed business builder. An avid student and lifelong learner, Dave has studied every major sales, marketing, or influence professional in the past 20 years. He's a master practitioner of Neuro-Linguistic Programming (NLP) who has studied with NLP's founder Richard Bandler and a graduate and former adjunct faculty of The Wizard of Ads Academy. You can book Dave for speaking engagements by calling (208) 863-8298.

Dave lives in Boise, Idaho, with his wife Stephanie and his daughter Austria. When not on the road with clients or speaking, Dave enjoys scuba diving, skiing, martial arts, reading, and great wine. Visit Dave online at www.howtopersuade.com.

Dave Lakhani is available for speaking engagements and corporate training seminars. To schedule Dave call 208-863-8298.

MANIPULATION

Love comes when manipulation stops; when you think more about the other person than about his or her reactions to you. When you dare to reveal yourself fully. When you dare to be vulnerable.

—Dr. Joyce Brothers

I n the Preface of this book I briefly described the religious cult I grew up in and how it was my impetus to study persuasion. When I began to study, the first realization I had was that while there were many similarities between manipulation and persuasion, the more I studied, the more I realized that manipulation is actually one path to persuasion, but only a temporary persuasion, not a lasting agreement.

The *American Heritage Dictionary* definition of *manipulation*, "Shrewd or devious management, especially for one's own advantage," is most fitting when discussing the difference between persuasion and manipulation. In manipulation the only person who benefits long term is the manipulator. Now look at the definition of the word *persuade*: "To induce to undertake a course of action or embrace a point of view by means of argument, reasoning, or entreaty." By persuading, there is the opportunity for two people to come together on an opinion that is mutually beneficial.

Manipulation is inwardly focused on the person who is manipulating. The manipulator is focused on achieving personal outcomes and goals with no concern for the outcome of or impact on the person being manipulated. Deception or covering up logical, factual evidence is also inherent in most manipulation, as demonstration or presentation of the facts would typically allow a rational person to come to a logical decision unfavorable to the manipulator.

Manipulation also strives to set up an artificial series of conditions or rules that govern the encounter so the manipulation can continue. There are typically penalties for challenging manipulators that can range from more deception to physical and emotional abuse to "shrewdly manage you for their own advantage." In discussing manipulation with noted psychologist Angela Dailey, she said, "Manipulation whether positive or negative is most clearly defined by the intent of the person who manipulates. If I tell a child who brings a bag of cookies from the cupboard just before bedtime and who intends to eat them all, that they can have one cookie or no cookies at all and they choose to have one cookie, I've created an illusion of choice but within the bounds of what I consider acceptable to me. I've manipulated the behavior, but for the good of the child who needs to get a full night of sleep."

In fact, discussion of manipulation with any psychology professional nearly always leads to the conclusion that the only real differentiator between manipulation and persuasion is intent. Robert Greene, author of *The 48 Laws of Power* (Penguin Putnam, 2001), was much clearer in his definition of manipulation. He said, "All attempts to influence are manipulation."

Nearly everyone has had an experience with being manipulated at one time or another. For many a common experience is that of buying a used car. While I certainly do not lump all used-car salespeople into the same category, it is an experience most of us have shared at one point in our life. So let's look at the setup that allows us to be manipulated.

Over Sunday brunch you and your spouse decide it is time to buy a new car. You want something newer than you have, but you don't want to spend the money for a brand-new model year car, so as you eat, you hear those magic words on the television from an overweight, mutton-chopped used-car salesman, "Come on down *Sunday, Sunday, Sunday,* to the Car Corral where prices are being slashed to the bone because we have inventory we must move. Our loss is your gain, but you must come down *today!*" You are a smart person; you look at your spouse, smile, and say, "Can't hurt to go down and look since they are having a sale; besides, there is no way that guy will get me to buy something I don't want." And so the first condition for manipulation (and persuasion) is met and that condition is: *the search for a solution.*

The search for a solution is very important to the manipulator and the persuader because searchers have lowered their defenses somewhat; they've indicated that they want something they don't have and they need specific knowledge, products, or services that you do have. The person being manipulated has an open mind to the possibility of what might be. By lowering their defenses and by opening themselves up to the idea that information exists they are not privy to, but need in order to achieve their goals, searchers willingly allow others to challenge their beliefs and to educate them in new possibilities. They've also set themselves up to be susceptible to the second condition: *time sensitivity.*

Time sensitivity is very important because we all have a very acute sense of time. Things must happen quickly, decisions must be made rapidly, and everyone knows that the early bird gets the worm. Manipulators and, again, persuaders know that reinforcing time sensitivity while increasing time pressure pushes people closer to impulsive decisions. It also sets the groundwork for the third condition for manipulation to work: *potential for loss.*

So, you walk onto the car lot thinking you are in charge, when in reality you are positioning yourself to be led. You meet your car salesman, and in the initial conversation with you, the car salesman demonstrates a very deep knowledge of cars. He is concerned that he understand what your real needs are so that he can demonstrate the most appropriate choices for you, since there is no way you can know everything there is to know about every car, but he can; after all, that is his job. The fourth condition is met: *encounter with a benevolent authority.*

While all four conditions are ideal for manipulation or persuasion, it is the intent of the person who is doing the manipulating or persuading that will determine what happens to you and ultimately to them and the business. There is one more condition that must be met and it is critical to success. We'll discuss that condition shortly.

In your bad experience with buying a used car, all four conditions aligned and you were not even consciously aware how susceptible you were to what would come next. As you shopped, you were likely told about a number of different options, but only one that was right for you. You were assured that no matter what your concern, there was a reasonable explanation as to why it was truly not a concern. Reassurances were given and backed up with technical-sounding information and demonstrations that were plausible; so you decided to buy.

This isn't the first time around the car-buying block, so when the time comes you hit them with your offer. The salesman sweats and says there is no way he can sell the car to you for what you offered, so he goes to see what he can do and talks it over with his manager. He comes back with another offer, this one lower than the sticker price but still above yours. He also lets you know at this point that one of the other salesmen has a customer who has already made an offer higher than yours, but has not signed the contract yet. You feel a little nervous and wonder if this is a sales trick. If it is, you will pay too much; if it isn't, you will lose the car, which is rapidly becoming the perfect car. This process repeats several times until finally the salesman comes back with a number higher than you want to pay, but he has some additional things he will "throw in" for you, some new tires and a CD player. It is the best he can do but you have to act now. If you walk off the lot, either the other buyer gets your car or you lose all the incentives to buy now. You are smart, though, so you decide to wait. You want to think it over for a couple of hours, so you get them to commit to the price and options if you call back by close of business, which they do unless the other buyer comes back in; then there is just nothing they can do.

Now it is late afternoon, the sun is about to sink behind the clouds for the day, and you decide you do want the car. The final condition for manipulation is met—you've *fully committed*. By committing mentally and emotionally, you have set yourself up for great loss, but you must have the car. The smart persuader and shrewd manipulator already got you to make some small commitments along the way and those are the ideas that push you over the edge. Sure there are a few nagging doubts, but it is a good deal and you bargained hard.

You call back and tell them you want the car and much to your dismay it is gone; the other salesman got his customer who was already willing to pay more to buy *your* car. You are dejected, you feel down; that was *your* car, you wanted it; if only you hadn't waited; now you have to start the process again knowing you may have let the very best deal slip through your fingers. You ask about other cars and the salesman is very willing to help if you want to come back in tomorrow. So you do.

When you arrive at the lot the next morning you are met by the salesman, who has incredible news: Financing fell through for the people who were going to buy *your* car and you can get it if you buy it now before they have time to qualify with another higher-risk lender. You are hooked and you buy the car *as is* immediately; you don't want to lose this car again; that was just too close.

You drive the car off the lot, and the next morning you wonder if you made a good decision; but it *is* a good-looking car, even the neighbor said so. A few days later you begin to notice a lot of little things you couldn't have noticed in a 10-minute test drive. As you begin to make mental notes of what is happening, you start trying to get in touch with the salesman. Your calls go unreturned. You drive it down to the lot and are summarily told that all sales are final but that they will be happy to have their service person look it over. They look it over and you find out that you will have to spend several hundred dollars to get the car fixed. Now you don't have a choice. If you want the car to work right you have to fix it; if you don't you face even bigger, more expensive problems later. And so begins your wonderful new car purchase. You feel cheated, suckered, and wonder how you got sucked in.

The good news is that it is not just you who is susceptible to the manipulator; we all are. The easy story, charismatic manner, and the setup are all but irresistible to most people. But that doesn't make you feel any better, does it? In fact, most people who are manipulated report feeling angry, hopeless, and not in control. The manipulator, on the other hand, had all needs met.

Manipulation works in the short term only because there is a lack of experience, information, or critical thought on the part of the person being manipulated. The moment you begin to critically think about the sequence of events or the occasion where you were manipulated, you begin to see all of the warning signs that were present during the interaction. So why didn't you pick up on them then? The answer is quite simple. When we are searching for solutions, any solution that seems to work tends to be the correct one. We find ways to justify or "force fit" the solution to the problem (or desire) that we have. Manipulators know that if they show you the solution, the way, the answer to your problem, you will immediately begin to rationalize any objections you have; you will find a way to make it fit. And, the shrewd manipulator will continue to layer on proof, emotion, and increase the pressure to take action now until you do. "The 80/20 rule applies very strongly in this situation," says psychologist Angela Dailey. "It is very easy to negate the 20 percent of doubt when it is overwhelmed by a more significant sense of desire or evidence, even when the doubt hangs around in the back of your mind. You find ways to justify or rationalize away the doubt so you can move back into your comfort zone."

Fortunately, nearly all manipulation is ultimately discovered and the manipulator is exposed. Many people, though not all, share their experiences with those around them. In extreme cases, the media pick up the story and thousands if not millions learn of the person and process and can therefore avoid it.

Manipulation does not work in the long run because there can be no ongoing trust or relationship with the manipulator. Deceptions are ultimately exposed and incongruence is observed and reconciled. Many times legal action of one form or another results. So the manipulators must find another target where word-of-mouth reputation won't catch up or be exposed at such a high level that they lose all creditability. Unfortunately, many people go on to be manipulated again because the perceived value of what they may receive is higher than the pain of being manipulated. Ultimately the pattern continues, not because they don't recognize the manipulator, but because the risk/potential reward ratio is high enough to outweigh critical thinking on the issue.

I am going to demonstrate the manipulation process for you so that you can see all of the elements. Please understand that I do not condone manipulation in any form, but do believe it is important for you to know how manipulation works so you do not become a victim and so that you do not unwittingly and unethically manipulate anyone.

How to Manipulate

1. Carefully observe your audience; look for people who are genuinely searching, who are looking for answers, salvation, and yet who are artificially confident or unsure.
2. Test their knowledge and their commitment. Find out how interested they really are in you and your subject. Ask a lot of questions, get them to tip their hand about how much knowledge they really have on the subject, then offer some

information that is not wrong, but questionable or contest-able. See if they challenge you in return. Present your infor-mation in a way that is sure and confident; present yourself as an expert.

3. Use broad, sweeping generalities and common-knowledge statements that encompass the common knowledge around the subject. Get them to agree with you.

4. Build your relationship, create trust, befriend them, and deepen your rapport.

5. Get them to verbalize their desire and commitment. Put them into a future situation where they have benefited from follow-ing your advice.

6. Begin to make them aware of what a great opportunity you are presenting them, but subtly. Build up the emotional desire for the idea you are presenting but let them understand that this is an opportunity that won't last forever. If possible, take the opportunity away from them once, but through a very reason-able set of circumstances; give them one last opportunity to get what you are promoting but make it contingent on making a decision right now.

7. Reinforce your relationship again as they leave.

8. If they start confronting you, place the blame for the prob-lem elsewhere. Blame the boss; tell them about your very sick grandmother and how you are really out of sorts today because of all the problems she is having that you have to take care of. Ask if they have ever experienced anything similar and ask for their advice or assistance; pull them in closer.

9. Continue the process until they are fully committed or until they stop coming back. If they commit, let them into the insiders' circle, the exclusive group for the ordained ones; give

them access to information or activities that no one else has access to. Help them in little ways when you can so their reliance on you increases and then offer them more opportunities to do what you want them to do.

🤝 Chapter Review

☛ Intent is the only clearly definable element that separates manipulation from persuasion.

☛ Manipulation is *inwardly* focused on the outcome for the person doing the manipulation. Persuasion is *externally* focused on developing a win-win outcome where everyone's needs are met.

☛ The four most important elements that must exist to manipulate or be manipulated are: seeking a solution, time sensitivity, potential for loss, and benevolent authority.

☛ Manipulation is effective only in the short term because nearly always the manipulator and the manipulative techniques will be revealed by an outside observer or through critical thinking.

☛ Manipulation is nearly always inappropriate in any situation, particularly in business and sales situations. If you want to earn a significant income and have a long career, you'll always avoid manipulation.

☛ Remember that short-term manipulation will never lead to long-term success when it comes to influencing people. The world is too small. Manipulators are always discovered.

 ## Success Questions

☞ What is my intention when I set out to persuade?
☞ What examples of having been manipulated in my personal life exist for my critical review?
☞ Are there any other differences between (or justifications for) persuading and manipulating?

2

PERSUASION

When I tell the truth, it is not for the sake of convincing those who do not know it, but for the sake of defending those that do.
—William Blake

This chapter on persuasion is not very long, because it is really a brief follow-up to the previous chapter and an opening for the rest of the book, which is all about persuasion and how to make it work. My purpose for this chapter is to demonstrate that there are some differences between persuasion and manipulation, but they are mostly internal differences—internal to you. You must make a decision, before you convince anyone of anything, about whether what you are doing is reasonable, ethical, legal, and moral. If the answer to even one of those criteria is no, then you should not do it.

Persuasion when done correctly is beautiful. It is much like watching a carefully orchestrated ballet. Every part of the process is unique unto itself yet by necessity a part of every other.

Persuasion is so closely related to manipulation that it is often hard for people to draw a distinct line. Most of the elements of manipulation must be in place for successful persuasion to happen, but the key difference is the intent of the person persuading.

In the first chapter we talked about a bad used-car-buying experience and yet nearly all of us have had a good car-buying experience as well. In the good experience the person selling you the car was truly as interested in helping you achieve your needs as you were in fulfilling your needs.

Later we look at the Persuasion Equation, which shows how you tie all of the elements of persuasion together consistently to achieve a predictable outcome each time you set out to get what you want.

Good persuasion is a practiced art, a carefully orchestrated dance between you and the person you are persuading. That orchestration involves understanding the true needs and desires of the person you are persuading, understanding his or her criteria for action, and finally presenting information in a way that is congruent with his or her indicated desires.

Manipulators spend a great deal of time creating a façade, but persuaders create a persona, a carefully crafted part of themselves that allows them to interact with others from a position of power and influence. A persuasive persona is an accepted part of who the person is. They actively and consciously develop that part for the purpose of getting more of what they want quickly and ethically, in any situation.

The best persuaders are innately curious about the world around them and the people they interact with. They want to know what makes the other guy tick. They are interested in the desires, dreams, and goals of the person they are persuading for the purpose of using those as leverage, to be sure, but equally to create a long-term relationship based in mutual respect. Persuasion is as much about learning what the other person needs on a physical level (product), as well as on an emotional level, and why, as it is about providing the right product or service at the right price. The best product or service at the best price presented poorly and in a way that is incongruent with the buyer's needs will often be overcome by an inferior product or price presented persuasively.

Persuasion is not just about selling, though; it is also about gaining agreement and support. It is about creating a common ground upon which two or more people can come together in thought and belief. Persuasion occurs in virtually every area of life, from what you have for breakfast to who makes it for you every morning. Virtually every aspect of our lives involves persuading someone (even ourselves) to do the things that we want him or her to do so we can have more of what we want.

Persuasion is an art form that improves through practice. No one is born a powerful persuader (though as I write this, my 10-month-old daughter has persuaded me to stop in mid-sentence and give her what she wants without saying a word). In order to be an effective persuader, you must take the time to learn about what makes people make the decisions they make. Fortunately, by the time you finish this book you will have learned all you need to know to be effective in persuading in any situation. However, simply reading this book won't be enough; you have to analyze your current persuasion process and yourself to see where you can improve. You also need to determine where in the process you overlay each of the principles that you are about to learn. Finally, you need to practice. You have to test the insertion of certain techniques or ideas into your current presentation process and study the feedback to understand how to use them more effectively for the fastest and best result.

Chapter Review

☞ Persuasion is about creating an environment that lets two or more people find common ground and belief.

☞ The fine line between persuasion and manipulation revolves around intent.

☞ Connotation also has a lot to do with how each of the two events is interpreted. Typically persuasion has a very positive connotation while manipulation does not.

 Success Questions

☞ What are my personal beliefs about when something is persuasive and when it is manipulative?

☞ How have my beliefs about the two supported me or held me back to date?

☞ How can I become more curious about the world around me and challenge my beliefs to come up with a broader knowledge and experience base from which to launch my persuasive arguments?

PERSONA—
THE INVISIBLE PERSUADER

My professional persona never loosens its grip, keeping an eye on me at all times.

—Agnetha Faltskog

Persuasion is like building a house. Your persona, which is the person you are, the person everyone will see and interact with, is the foundation and the walls of the house. Persona gives your persuasiveness structure and support; it also holds the rest of the components that will give it beauty, desirability, warmth, and safety.

In order to be persuasive your persona must be developed to fully support your message. You must look the part, sound the part, and act the part. If your message and your persona are not congruent, people you hope to persuade may make an unfavorable decision about you.

Current research reveals that people make decisions nearly instantaneously. They don't need overwhelming information to "thin slice" what they see and make a decision. Malcolm Gladwell, in his exceptional book on how we think, called *Blink* (Little, Brown, 2005), discusses in detail how art experts are able to detect a forgery nearly the second they look at an object; long before they can conclusively explain why they know it is a forgery, they "thin slice" the information and make a decision. The same principle allows you and me to make decisions in the blink of an eye about whether someone is being honest, if she knows what she is talking about, and if she has our best intentions at heart.

There are three elements of your persona that you must focus on and develop in order to persuade at the highest levels:

1. Appearance
2. Voice and communication skills
3. Positioning

Please understand when I talk about persona, I am not suggesting you develop a façade or mask to wear when you are trying to persuade; rather I am talking about fully developing a positive set of skills that become an integral part of your personality. You may employ the skills more or less throughout the day, but you will always employ them fully when you are persuading. As you become more adept at persuading and as you practice the skills more and more, they will soon become an unconscious part of you that you automatically apply in the appropriate situations.

APPEARANCE

People judge you by your appearance. Studies have proven over and over that tall men do better than short men on job interviews and when dating. Attractive people are more likely to be hired than their less attractive peers when equally qualified. A very detailed study of attractiveness was published in the American Psychological Association's *Psychological Bulletin,* called "What is beautiful is good, but . . . : A meta-analytic review of research on the physical attractiveness stereotype," by Alice H. Eagly, Richard D. Ashmore, Mona G. Makhijani, and Laura C. Longo in 1991. This very interesting study is worthwhile for every serious student of persuasion.

While this all sounds incredibly unfair, it is a simple fact of life. As human beings we make instant judgments about other human beings based on many different criteria, and attractiveness is one of them. The good news is that no matter how you look today, you can tilt the playing field in your favor rather easily; but you must make a conscious effort to do so.

You must aggressively and honestly evaluate your appearance today. I want you to ask yourself a few simple questions and answer them honestly; these questions apply equally to men and women. In the last 12 months have you:

- ☞ Evaluated or updated your hairstyle?
- ☞ Looked at all of the clothes you wear daily for signs of wear?
- ☞ Gained or lost more than 10 pounds?
- ☞ Replaced shirts or blouses that you wear more than two to three times a month?
- ☞ Had your shoes professionally polished regularly?
- ☞ Evaluated your clothing choices and styles to see if they are still current or appropriate to your position?
- ☞ Closely examined your face, head, and ears for signs of aging, sun damage, or errant hairs that need to be removed?

☞   If you are a man, carefully examined your haircut to see if it supports your hairline?

☞   If you are a woman, carefully evaluated your style and color to see if it is making you look age appropriate or slightly younger?

☞   Evaluated your clothing to be sure there are no holes or worn or frayed areas?

☞   Gotten rid of items in your wardrobe that you haven't worn in 12 months? (If you haven't worn it in 12 months, it is very unlikely you ever will again or that the style will be appropriate or in fashion.)

☞   Taken a close look at how your hands and fingernails look?

It may seem simplistic, perhaps vain to go through a checklist like this, but you must remember that every person you are hoping to persuade is evaluating everything about you. It is not the large, obvious things you do wrong that make persuasion difficult. For example, if you lie and are caught, the relationship is over. It is the smaller, less obvious clues we don't pay attention to that people pick up on subconsciously and that can make persuasion difficult. They have an internal expectation, a map, and when there is a mismatch in the information you provide and the information they expect, they hesitate or they disconnect entirely.

As human beings we are constantly subconsciously evaluating hundreds of pieces of information at once and making decisions about them outside of consciousness. Only those things that are surprising or extremely incongruent get our conscious attention—the rest are evaluated, and decisions made, in the background. That is exactly why you have a nagging feeling about situations that do not seem right but you can't put your finger on precisely what is "off." Sometimes we call this intuition. In reality, it is a very detailed subconscious process that allows us to make dozens of decisions at once. In order to persuade effectively we must pay careful attention to every piece of information we present to our audience if we hope to get our message into the internal pattern that says this person is knowledgeable and trustworthy. You want your audience to think, "I should continue this interaction."

Each of us has an expectation about how someone should look or act or sound in every situation we are in. Imagine for a moment if your doctor were also a farmer and he walked in from the farm in his muddy boots and jeans with a beatup ball cap on and told you that you had cancer but he was there to help you find the best way to treat it. Would he have a lot of credibility with you? Would he have rapport? Would you be forced to consciously evaluate his position and would you be more or less likely to take his advice? Granted, much would depend on the relationship you already had with that doctor, but even if the relationship was perfect, his demeanor and persona would not match the internal pattern you have about how a doctor should look and act.

By carefully evaluating yourself using the checklist, you will be able to see yourself the way others see you. Once you have evaluated your appearance, you can quickly change those items that require action to present the image your clients, prospects, or potential partners expect.

Dressing Persuasively

There is an interesting breadth of opinions when it comes to how you should dress to interact with clients. Many of the executives I spoke with said they would never want their employees to dress better than their prospects or clients. Others felt that wearing a suit or at least a blazer at all times was appropriate. Still others held that a company uniform (logo shirt and slacks) was always appropriate. One executive even told me he felt that dressing worse than your prospects or clients made the clients feel as if they were doing better and that you were not spending all their money on clothes. That is wrong! The purpose of clothes is to support your position and to draw attention to you, but not to the clothes themselves.

Maybe one of the most overlooked benefits of dressing persuasively is how it makes you feel. Whenever you put on certain kinds of clothes you begin to feel differently emotionally and physically. Wearing a nice suit that fits well makes you feel great, able, and ready. Some people feel uncomfortable when they dress up because they are not used to it. All the more reason to dress better regularly, so you get used to the feeling and it becomes a congruent part of who you are.

Ultimately the rule of thumb you should follow to be effectively persuasive is this: Dress as someone in your position is expected to dress or as well as your client or one step better. What does one step better mean? If your client dresses in business casual (universally, every image consultant I talked with said jeans were *not* business casual), then adding a tie and a blazer would be an example of one step up. Or, adding a third layer to your business casual, which could mean a vest or some kind of jacket for men, or a sweater or scarf for women. The idea is not to become incongruent, but to set yourself apart slightly so you command attention.

In addition, you need to dress appropriately for the environment. If you sell fertilizer on a farm and you are meeting a farmer in the field to evaluate soil, it doesn't make any sense to show up in a suit; in fact, it brings your credibility and knowledge into immediate question, much like the doctor in the earlier example.

Dressing as well as your client means wearing an expected style of clothes that are clean, pressed, and current in their style. Nonnegotiable issues are these: Your shoes must always be polished, your nails neatly groomed, your clothes freshly pressed, and your hairstyle current, including the cut. If you are wearing a company shirt or other uniform, it should be clean and neatly pressed. If you travel by car most of the day and wear a company uniform of some kind it will likely become very wrinkled by midday. Changing into a crisply pressed shirt halfway through your in-person appointments, if possible, will keep you looking sharp.

Your clothes must also fit. If your clothes fit you well they cover flaws in your body and look nice and move well, and you feel good in them, resulting in a higher level of self-confidence. If you have gained or lost more than 10 pounds, it's likely your clothes are beginning to fit poorly. Anything over 10 pounds may require alteration or temporary replacement. If you are debating this idea right now, ask yourself this: Would you expect a client to buy a product that looked bad or was damaged in some way without questioning the quality or validity of the product? If the answer is no, then don't ask them to buy you when you look questionable.

While there have been many great guides written on what to wear, none of them really looks at how what you wear influences your ability to be authoritative or persuasive. Recently I met Judith Rasband, CEO of Conselle Institute of Image Management in Provo, Utah, and she has solved the problem. Rasband is the inventor of the Style Scale. She developed the scale so people could very quickly and easily determine what their wardrobe was saying or what they wanted to say with their wardrobe. Image is ranked on a scale of 0–4, 0 being low authority and 4 being high authority. Authority corresponds very nicely to persuasion. For example, in level 4, high authority, men would wear matched suit trousers and suit jacket with shirt and tie. When dressing, the more stark the contrast between the suit and shirt (black suit/white shirt), and the more angular the lines, the more authoritarian the appearance. For women, level 4 would be suit skirt and suit jacket with shirt or blouse; dress and jacket; or pantsuit slacks and jacket with shirt. Level 3 for men would be slacks and a sport coat with shirt and tie, and for women, skirt or slacks, with jacket and shirt or blouse. Level 2 for women would include skirt and shirt with collar, with sweater or vest; skirt and shirt with collar, or Polo shirt; or pants and shirt with collar. Level 2 for men would include pants with collared shirt and tie, with a sweater or vest. Finally, level 1 for a man would be jeans and T-shirt, shorts and T-shirt or sleeveless shirt, and for women, jeans and T-shirt, sleeveless tops, shorts, and sundresses. For most persuasive environments, levels 3 or 4 will be appropriate. Rarely will level 1 be appropriate unless you are trying to convince your neighbor to help you move!

Here are a few final tips to make your appearance really stand out:

- ☞ Your socks should always match or be a shade darker than your hem.
- ☞ Facial hair for men is acceptable but must always be neatly groomed.

☞ Haircuts for men or women should be stylish and well-groomed.

☞ Jewelry should be worn minimally and should support the overall look without detracting.

☞ Suits do not have to be cleaned every time you wear them. Simply hang them over the back of a chair and allow them to air before you rehang them. Unless the suit has an odor or stain, simply have it pressed regularly and cleaned approximately two to three times a year.

☞ All clothing should be neatly pressed regularly.

☞ Men's shoes and belt should match.

☞ When buying level 3 or level 4 clothes, buy the best pieces you can reasonably afford; they will look better and last longer.

☞ Have all of your level 3 and level 4 clothes tailored to properly fit your frame and shape.

One question that always arises is whether to wear custom or off-the-rack clothing. The answer really depends a lot on you, and as it turns out, the majority of people can't tell the difference by looking at your clothes. I spoke with Steve Reeder of Tom James Inc., one of the nation's largest manufacturers of custom and ready-made clothing, and he had this to say: "Men and women alike will most benefit from custom shirts. Unless you have a shape that is hard to fit or you simply like the look and feel of a custom-made suit of clothing, there are many wonderful ready-made pieces that can be tailored to fit you nicely that will look wonderful, wear well, and cost hundreds if not thousands less than custom suits of clothes." The key to success is in finding a good tailor and purchasing quality clothing that can be taken in and out and tailored to fit you perfectly.

VOICE AND COMMUNICATION SKILLS

The moment someone sees you he begins to make decisions about you. Those decisions are reinforced or brought into question the moment you speak. If you are not meeting face to face, your voice and communication skills are the very first information people receive in order to begin evaluating you. You don't need a radio announcer's voice and a television personality's presence to be successful, but you must know how to use your voice and your body to create a powerful, believable message. Your presentation skills must reinforce everything you say.

When it comes to your voice, remember that it sounds different to you than it does to everyone else. As you listen to your voice, you are hearing it inside your body, not outside. One of the most powerful things you can do today is to record your voice and see how it sounds to everyone listening to it. Now I know you will say, "I have heard my voice and I am not crazy about how it sounds on tape." The reality is that your voice is probably just fine; you simply need to learn how to use it properly in order to give it maximum impact.

In researching this topic I spoke with the nation's top voice coach, Susan Berkley. You may know Susan best as one of the voices that says "Thank you for using AT&T." Susan is also the author of *Speak to Influence—How to Unlock the Hidden Power of Your Voice*. Susan says the single biggest mistake people make in using their voices is that they do not project their voices, because they speak from someplace other than the facial mask. The facial mask is made up of the lips, mouth, and nose area. The best way to find your facial mask is to hum. As you hum, pay attention to where you feel the vibration in your facial area; that is the facial mask. To improve the way you speak simply hum a song you know and halfway through humming, start speaking the words. Try to have the words create the same feeling in the same place in your face as humming. Remember, unless you are a professional voiceover artist, you are not trying to sound like a radio DJ or other professional voice (which can be detrimental); you are simply maximizing the impact of the voice you have. There are a number of other exercises you can do to improve the quality of your voice, and as hackneyed as it sounds, every expert I talked to on improving your voice said smiling as you speak improves the quality and tone of your voice.

The speed at which you speak also has a great deal of impact on how persuasive you are. Varying the speed and pitch of your voice makes you interesting and desirable to listen to. If you speak too slowly or too quickly, you lose a lot of people. People who speak very slowly are often considered unsure or not as bright, and people who speak with a rapid-fire staccato are often considered to be scattered or high pressure. Both of those generalizations may be unfair and undeserved, but they are nonetheless the observations many in our society make. You give yourself significant advantage by listening to how you sound to others. Ask people who are colleagues, but not relatives, to honestly critique your voice. If there are significant challenges you feel you need to correct, or if you simply want to improve your voice overall, I strongly recommend a voice coach. Virtually anyone will sound better and more polished in just a few sessions.

In order to persuade more effectively, it is important to learn to vary your voice when you speak. Nearly everyone has had the experience of listening to someone drone on in a flat, monotone voice that has no emotion or, seemingly, life to it. Using a monotonous voice causes people to focus on your voice and delivery rather than the message you are trying to send. The purpose of your voice in persuasion is to deliver a message in a meaningful, understandable, and motivating way. Your message, not your voice, should be the focal point of the listener.

Think for a moment about the great speakers you have had the pleasure to hear (a motivational speaker, a minister, perhaps a comedian). Their voices vary with regularity to add impact to their messages. They mark out a specific thought or idea by changing the tone of their voice or the rate of speed at which they speak. Great speakers also use pauses for dramatic effect. When they want you to really understand or ponder, they pause before moving to the next point. Pauses are persuasive, providing a subconscious clue to the listener to give thought to the previous information or to pay attention because a change in thought is coming.

Persuasive speakers' patterns of speech are coherent and cohesive, and they work diligently to remove filler words like *and, uh, you know,* and the dozens of other little words we throw into our everyday speech where a pause would have served nicely and improved the power and effectiveness of the message. Work on developing a pattern or rhythm to your speech. It can be as simple as delivering your speech in a rhythm similar to counting the beats of music, or one that is more complex that copies the rhythm, tonality, pitch, and speed of the person you are speaking to. No matter your style, the most important element is to know what you plan to say before you say it and then deliver it with conviction. Your own natural persuasive pattern will emerge the moment you know your material cold.

For example, if I asked you to tell me about your job, you could easily give me a detailed description. Your story would flow from beginning to end, your breathing would be natural and smooth, and your voice would flow rhythmically up and down appropriately. On the other hand, if I asked you to describe how to deliver a baby, unless it is your job, it is very likely you would have a difficult time explaining it. You may know some of the elements but you would not be able to put them together in a format that would be persuasive. As you tried to describe how to deliver a baby, your sentences would be choppy; your voice would be stressed; your mouth would become somewhat dry, and your voice would be full of question and uncertainty, all of which the listener would easily detect.

Sometimes it is necessary to convince or persuade someone of something you are unprepared for. For example, you join a new organization and are chosen to be the person to go out and get merchandise for the silent auction fundraiser. So you gather basic information about the group based on what you know and what you have been told and begin your task. Especially when you have minimal knowledge, it is best to go over what you intend to say out loud a few times. Listen to how it sounds: Where do you get stuck, where do you pause, where are you unsure? Then, in all of those places: Slow down, breathe before you make the point, then speak clearly through the areas you have had trouble with; practice it a few times, then go. If you are really put on the spot, go through it in your head a few times before starting your presentation. Ideas that have been thought through even slightly come across much more clearly and convincingly in your voice than those you make up on the fly. You can nearly always tell someone who is making things up on the fly simply by listening to the rhythm and tone of his voice without hearing a word he is saying.

Do you want to improve your rhythm? Listen to audio books and pay careful attention to how the reader reads the story, or listen to poetry spoken aloud. Each gives you a very distinct view of how rhythm in communication should sound. Watching a live storyteller can also dramatically improve your ability to communicate orally. Finally, study actors who must sell you on the idea of their character each time you watch them. Listen to how they speak, how their emotions come through in their voices, how they lead you with the words they say, and how they use dramatic pauses for emphasis and to enhance the impact of a moment or feeling.

Very closely tied to voice is presentation. How you present your material will determine how successful you are in persuading. Whether you intend to speak to a group or will only influence people over the phone, you should have formal speech training. Toastmasters (www.toastmasters.org) is the most cost-effective and easily accessible program available. It is also very powerful because you get honest feedback from others just like you. An additional benefit I have discovered from Toastmasters is that you can try out new material and get very valuable feedback on both content and presentation before formally delivering it to your audience.

Speech training gives you a format for delivery of material whether you are using graphics and presenting to a large audience, presenting to small groups, or communicating one on one. Speech training goes much further than just helping you become a better speaker, as it gives you a methodology for successfully delivering your message. The most powerful persuaders are able to clearly and concisely present their message to anyone in a well-organized and understandable way. As of this writing, maybe the most notable person who should be highly polished as a persuasive presenter, political beliefs aside, is President George Bush. He is clearly well educated and the most powerful leader in the world, yet his ability to present information certainly hindered him during the elections and throughout his first term and, it appears, will continue to plague him through his second term. Contrast Bush's style to that of President Bill Clinton, who was a very articulate and polished speaker. He was able to deliver his message in a way that appeared genuine, honest, and thoughtful, and, even when under the most difficult scrutiny, he got people on his side. While I'm certain President Bush has many people working with him to improve his appearance and presentation, very simple changes on his part would make him more believable and effective.

There are a few key points to keep in mind before you present your material that will make your persona more complete and you instantly more persuasive.

- ☞ Always look at the person to whom you are speaking. If you are presenting to a group, look at different individuals throughout your presentation.
- ☞ Try to make your presentation interactive—get the person or audience to ask or answer questions.
- ☞ Say your words completely. If there is a *g* on the end, say it: it's *thinking*, not thinkin'.
- ☞ Don't turn your back and speak over your shoulder or look over your shoulder to read. If you must read from a graphic or turn to demonstrate something, never turn more than 90 degrees away from your audience so your head can move

naturally back and forth between whatever you are demonstrating and your audience.

☞ Keep an open posture: Keep folded arms and barriers between you and your audience to a minimum.

☞ Use your body to reinforce your message. For example, use
wider, open-handed movements.

Whether you are presenting your message to the citizens of the
world or your five-person company, there is no good reason not to
work on polishing your persona and your presentation skills. Simply by being trustworthy, likable, and knowledgeable before you
speak your first word, you will gain the opportunity to start breaking down the barriers people erect to protect themselves not just
from unscrupulous manipulators, but also from those of us who
wish and even need to persuade them for their own good.

POSITIONING

Positioning is really all about bringing your persona together.
It is the final touches in your overall presentation that round
out the perception someone will have about you instantly. It is
your conscious effort to be seen as knowledgeable, helpful, committed, and sure all in one single glance. It is your ability to
present your persona in a way that anyone who doesn't know
you would make the most logical conclusion about you and
who you are . . . and that logical conclusion should be that
you are someone who can be trusted, respected, and looked to
for advice.

Your manners and mannerisms are a key factor in positioning.
Many times when people think about positioning, they are really
thinking about posturing. There is a real difference between the two

terms. Positioning is all about moving yourself authentically and ethically into a position of power with your audience. Posturing on the other hand may be artificial; you may back away from the position, or put it out there temporarily to see how people react. It also smacks a little of sucking up to others to get what you want.

When you dress appropriately, when you speak well and are polished in your presentation, you are positioning yourself to be seen and heard. You are also positioning yourself to be considered. I chose the word *considered* carefully because it is the most appropriate word; you want everyone who meets you to listen and consider what you have to say. If people think you are posturing or sucking up to them just to get something from them, they will immediately disengage from you. They may talk about you later, but it won't be in any way you hope they will. When people consider you and consider what you have to say, though, they have no choice but to give it deeper thought and review. They must evaluate your message from a deeper place to see if they agree with it intellectually and emotionally, and they give you the latitude to continue to provide them with additional pieces of information to persuade them, which they then compare to everything else you've said or done thus far.

When you think about positioning it is important to consider your mannerisms. The little things you do say a lot. One of the very best ways to look at your own mannerisms is to videotape yourself at work one day while you are talking on the phone and another day while you are speaking to a group. Observe yourself very closely, first with the sound up and then with the sound turned off. Have someone else watch with you for a few moments and ask them what they notice most about you. The things you notice and that others watching you notice are the things your audience, whether one or many, will remember about you.

Some of the most important things to watch out for are hand motions, particularly preening, cleaning, or nervous motions around your face. Use your hands to reinforce your message or keep them at your sides comfortably. Also notice how you stand and move. Do you slump, or stand upright and well balanced? Do you shift your weight back and forth or rock when you talk to people or groups? Do you make distracting noises or do anything else that draws attention away from you and to the mannerism? If so, work on correcting those. If you have a problem with your posture, start working on it, since correcting your posture and gait does not take long. If you do not know how, find a Feldenkrais practitioner (or book), a chiropractor, or kinesiologist who can take you through some very powerful but simple body mechanics exercises that will help you walk and stand in a flowing, balanced way.

Another area often overlooked in positioning is etiquette. Often when we persuade it is around the dining table, and for many of us, basic manners and principles of etiquette have gone unlearned or have been forgotten. While I am not going to attempt to write a whole chapter on etiquette (there are thousand-page books on the topic), I do want to point out the most obvious that enhance your persona and others' perception of you. In order to give you the most current and valuable tips I interviewed Mercedes Alfaro, CEO of First Impression Management, an etiquette and professional image management company. Here are her tips:

☞ When at the table, the bread plate on the left is yours, the water glass on the right is yours.
☞ The napkin goes in your lap when you sit down or when the host puts his in his lap.
☞ The napkin goes into your lap fold forward, away from your torso.

☞ It is a napkin, not a washrag; use it to wipe your fingers or mouth. Anything more requires a trip to the restroom.

☞ It is a napkin, not a tissue; no blowing—in fact, no nose-blowing at the table *ever*.

☞ If you need to clean yourself go to the restroom. That includes cleaning spills from your clothes.

☞ Pass things like the breadbasket and condiments before you help yourself.

☞ If you are the host you pay for the meal, period.

☞ If you are concerned about wrestling for the bill, arrive early and give your credit card to the waitstaff with instructions to bring the receipt to you at the conclusion of the meal.

☞ When seated, the person of highest importance gets the best seat at the table—the one with the best view.

☞ The person inviting another to a meal should recommend a restaurant, trying to discover food preferences ahead of the invitation when possible.

☞ Cell phones should be off or on vibrate—no answering or calling during the meal.

☞ Forks and spoons are always used with the left hand even if you are right-handed.

☞ The fork should never be held like a dagger with the tines coming out of the bottom of your hand. It should rest in the palm of your hand, the tines coming out between the thumb and forefinger. When the hand is closed and turned palm down, the curved back portion of the fork should rest just under your index fingertip.

☞ The knife should not be used as a saw. Use easy stroking motions, drawing the handle toward you. If you are having difficulty, ask for a sharper knife.

☞ Official etiquette rules state no business until the entrée dishes are cleared away. This is unfortunately not practical in most cases as you have limited time, particularly at lunch.

☞ A rule of thumb is to spend about one-third of the meal discussing nonbusiness issues, one-third discussing business, and the final third away from business again. Then, at the conclusion of the meal, recap the steps that each will take.

☞ Develop a good handshake. The pattern is palm to palm, web of thumb to web of thumb, and fingers wrapped around the other person's hand. Pump up and down two to three times. This applies equally to men and women.

☞ While it remains very traditionally good manners for a man to stand up when a woman arrives at or leaves the table, it is no longer a requirement, particularly in a business environment.

☞ If there is an issue with the food or the bill, do not address it at the table. Excuse yourself and talk to the waitstaff or manager as appropriate.

☞ Remember that not everyone has good manners or etiquette but they nearly always recognize it.

The persuasive persona does not consist of a few big things to make it work; it is all the little things you do right that add up to success. The power behind developing your persona is in guiding your audience to the conclusions you want them to draw and in getting them to trust you, respect you, and value you before you say a word. Let them be pulled in by your carefully crafted persona and let them remain enthralled by its depth, complexity, and completeness. If you make your persona one that they themselves would like to emulate, you have done your job perfectly.

Chapter Review

☛ Persona is the invisible persuader, working beneath conscious evaluation to help people make the instantaneous decisions that they will make about it in our favor.

☛ You must focus on the three core areas of persona to maximize success: appearance, voice and communication, and positioning.

☛ Use your voice to increase your power. Speak from the facial mask to project appropriately. Use vocal variety to underscore important points in your message and to make what you are saying more interesting.

☛ Dress at level 3 or 4 for most business situations for maximum persuasiveness. Be sure to check yourself in the mirror regularly to be sure your clothes and appearance support your image.

☛ Check your manners and mannerisms regularly. Let your polish set you apart from your competition.

☛ Position yourself for success in the eyes of those who matter most—the people you wish to persuade.

☛ Remember people are getting a message the moment they see you, before they hear a word you say. Be sure you are positioning yourself for maximum influence.

 Success Questions

☛ Have I gone through the checklists in this chapter and compared myself honestly?

☛ What is the message my appearance, voice, and positioning send today?

☛ What elements of my persona can I enhance immediately that will give me an edge?

☛ What elements of my persona are already very effective and how can I use that to my advantage?

☛ How can I learn to speak better to sound more professional and polished?

☛ What do I need to do to convince myself that my persona is the foundation of my persuasive success?

TRANSFERRING POWER AND CREDIBILITY

All credibility, all good conscience, all evidence of truth come only from the senses.

—Friedrich Nietzsche

The company you keep and the people who endorse you have a powerful effect on your ability to persuade. When someone like Donald Trump recommends a banker or a developer, that person is rarely questioned or challenged because of the implied or outright endorsement of Trump himself. You are also judged by the company you keep. People will make assumptions about you based on your friends and associates, which can be very powerful . . . or devastating depending on your group of friends and associations. For example, you may be more inclined to do business with someone who is a member of the Better Business Bureau or the Chamber of Commerce simply because of what those organizations stand for, particularly if you don't have experience in the category of business from which you are going to purchase a product or service.

Being able to have a strong lineup of people who will willingly endorse you or belonging to the right groups or associations is something everyone who persuades must consciously set out to develop. Take a look around you right now. It has been said that your net worth is determined by looking at the average net worth of your closest friends. In the same respect, your persuasive net worth can be determined by the people you choose to associate with. If you hope to excel as a persuader you should be actively involved with the most persuasive people and associations that you can that are closely related to those you hope to persuade. However, being a part of a group or having influential friends is not enough by itself. You must actively cultivate their endorsement, whether it is direct or implied.

TRANSFER OF POWER AND CREDIBILITY

Transfers of power happen every day in dozens of situations. You recommend your barber to your neighbor and he starts doing business with that barber; you want to get into the best doctor in town so you have your friend drop a good word for you. You want a good job so you give your very best reference. In each of these examples there was an active transfer of power, some more overt than others, but in each one person went to bat for the other, actively saying, "You can trust this person because I say so and you trust me."

When my wife was pregnant we wanted the best ob-gyn in town and he was not taking any new clients, period. He was treating a very good friend's wife who had just had a baby and who was also the campaign manager for one of our senators. When she mentioned that we'd really like to get in, he immediately made room on his calendar for us. Why? Because it wasn't that he didn't have room for more patients, it was that he only had room for more of the kind of patients he was looking for. Because he knew my friend's wife, he was more than happy to fit us in. We went through nearly the same process with our pediatrician.

Active Power and Credibility Transfer

Active transfers of power typically happen when one person asks another to endorse her or vouch for her in some way. Active transfers can also happen when someone you've just met introduces you to peers or colleagues. That individual is putting his relationship and credibility on the line for the person he is introducing or endorsing.

All too often we miss the opportunity to get active transfers of power because we are afraid to ask, yet that simple transfer of power and credibility from me to you makes persuasion much easier and much more effective. A more applicable example in business would be asking for referrals and having the person whom you want to refer you actually introduce you in person or by phone and give his endorsement of you at the time. The likelihood is much higher that the person to whom you've just been introduced will buy from you because of the relationship she has with her friend, the endorser.

One of the nonprofit groups I have worked with in the past solicits donations door to door. I had them make one simple change in their process. Rather than just asking which of their neighbors might be interested in helping, I asked them when we walked to that neighbor's if they would simply wave to the neighbor when they came to the door. That simple act of waving increased donations by over 15 percent. The endorsement was overt, but not one word was exchanged. And the person who was asking for the donation simply said to the neighbor, "I just came from your neighbor's house and they said you are a great person to talk to."

Take the time right now to make a list of all the people you know who could help you in some situation where you are required to persuade on a regular basis and ask them if they will introduce you to at least one person you would like to persuade. If they will give you an outright endorsement that is even better, but if they won't or if they are not currently a client of yours, simply have them make the introduction. Once the introduction is made persuasion becomes significantly easier. The people you hope to persuade will make assumptions about you and your worthiness to do business with them based simply on an introduction. But beware, they may go back to the person who introduced you and confirm information. Be sure what you say about the relationship you have with the person is accurate.

Another often-overlooked transfer of power is testimonials. When one CEO tells another CEO of a similar company that one supplier is better than another, that supplier's chance of winning business improves. The same is true when you have written testimonials or if you are putting them on your web site, audio, or video promotions. Those transfers of power cut right to the heart of my concern. The reason I am concerned about what you are telling me may be because I don't know you or I have no experience with you, but when someone else steps up metaphorically and says he trusts you, I begin to get more comfortable. And, with each additional testimonial I get more comfortable.

Finally, anytime you can get someone who is actively transferring power and credibility to actually demonstrate how something works or share her results with your product or service, you increase the transfer. She is in effect not just giving you her power and credibility but is in fact persuading for you, which is the ultimate transfer of power and credibility.

Implied Transfer of Power and Credibility

Implied transfers of power happen when people listen to what you say based on what they believe about people, places, events, organizations, or shared experiences.

The organizations you belong to have a lot of power, prestige, and trust associated with them as well. Organizations that can be particularly powerful are fraternities, fraternal organizations (Masons, Elks, Shriners), business organizations (Chamber of Commerce, Better Business Bureau, Jaycees, Rotary, Young Presidents Organization), nonsecular organizations (churches, synagogues, Christian Businessmen's Associations), and charities (American Red Cross, Make A Wish Foundation). Even informal organizations like Neighborhood Watch give you an opportunity to associate with people who will be more willing to listen to what you say and trust you based on your shared experiences or shared commitment to a set of ideas or principles. When you talk to other people inside the organization there is trust because you are alike; when you talk to those outside the organization there is a degree of trust based on their experience and belief about the organization.

Other implied transfers of power and credibility happen when you are the subject of media coverage. This is why as a persuader you must have a personal public relations plan. With some notable exceptions, people believe more of what they see, read, or hear because there is an assumption that if it is in print or on the news, then it must be true. We can all point to many times when the news was wrong, yet we continue to watch and believe. We pay more attention to the cars that we see featured in newscasts and we trust products that have been covered. We also trust and listen to those people who end up on the news because they wouldn't be there if they were not experts on their subject. There is room for everyone in the news: As of this writing, more than 50 percent of what you see in the news is not hard news, but is placed or developed by publicists working to effectively position products and people. Always remember to try to get the person who is interviewing you or writing about you active in giving his endorsement or testimonial. Even if he hasn't tried your product or service, use powerful questions to move him to acknowledge that he intends to try it, and the transfer of power and credibility is made. You can make your own news, too. We talk about that more in Chapter 6.

There are many other times when transfers of credibility can be important. For example, in negotiations, simply having someone who is neutral or who is respected transfer her credibility to your argument can make your position more acceptable or make you appear more reasonable. When you are writing e-mails or sending letters, you can transfer credibility by copying the person whose authority or credibility you want on the e-mail or on the correspondence.

Power and credibility transfers are reciprocal. If you want people to endorse you, then be the first to endorse. Be known for your willingness to help people make the connections they need so they are indebted to you and will help you make the connections that are important to you. Also be very careful how you use the credibility that has been transferred to you. You alienate two people the moment you mistreat a person whose trust has been given to you: the mistreated person and the person who endorsed you.

 Chapter Review

☞ Transfers of power and credibility from a respected or trusted person to you enhance your ability to persuade.

☞ Transfers of power and credibility can be active or implied.

☞ Active transfers of power and credibility can happen in person or through testimonials.

☞ Implied transfers of power occur when people make decisions about you based on the company you keep and the organizations you belong to.

☞ Give to receive. Be known for the company you keep and your willingness, when appropriate, to transfer your own power and credibility in order to get the transfer when you need it.

 Success Questions

☞ Whom do I know today who can transfer power or credibility to me in a situation I am currently trying to influence?

☞ Whom do I know who needs my power or influence?

☞ What organizations could I or should I belong to that will enhance my ability to persuade by giving me implied power and/or credibility?

☞ How can I use testimonials or other endorsements to help me persuade more effectively?

5

STORYTELLING

I keep six honest serving-men
(They taught me all I knew);
Their names are What and Why and
When and How and Where and Who.
> —Rudyard Kipling, "The Elephant's Child,"
> *Just So Stories*

There is nothing quite as compelling or fascinating as a story well told. You must listen—you are drawn in and completely engaged.

When I was a young boy I had only a couple of places to go for refuge. The Carnegie Library in Caldwell, Idaho, was my favorite. The Carnegie was one of the last of its kind in my part of Idaho. It was a big stone building that sat on a stately lawn shaded by large trees and was covered randomly in ivy. It was somehow imposing and inviting at the same time. Something odd happened each time I walked by the library. It opened its arms and beckoned me in with irresistible force, wrapping me in its bookish embrace the moment the heavy door swung closed. Once I got inside I entered a whole new world, a world inhabited by Ernest Hemingway, Jack Kerouac, Zane Grey, Peter Hathaway Capstick, Jack London, Robert Ruark, Louis L'Amour, and Mark Twain. Each of these men was a willing participant in my protection and education. They gleefully took me to faraway lands where I met interesting people and had unbelievable adventures with them. Each of them taught me how to tell a story in a new and unique way and each of them introduced me to someone else desirous of expanding my mind and my experience. They taught me how to see a story everywhere and they showed me how to share it with you.

As I write this, I am sitting in Minneapolis, Minnesota. It is 25 degrees below zero outside and as I watch the people rushing below my hotel window, I see their faces buried deep in their coats and scarves . . . all but one peculiar man, that is; his exposed skin is blast-furnace red, his hair is freezer burned, and his painful breath is exhaled in cartoon balloons that break off and crash, shattering into the street. As I watch him, I realize that he is in trouble. I can tell without hearing a word he is cursing and his fists flail frantically. Little does he know his predicament is about to get worse; he can't see it coming, but I can.

See how difficult it is to stop reading the story? Right now you are left wondering what happens next, you want to know, you have to know. With a few simple sentences, I broke through your reverie and caused you to have an experience. You know what 25 degrees below feels like, or you have a very good idea. I bet even as you read this you can imagine the chill going down your spine and breathing in air so cold it freezes your nose and burns your lungs. And I am sure you can imagine this poor man and wonder what is about to happen to him. So before I teach you anything else, let me tell you what unfolded in front of my eyes.

The man pounds the glass in front of him hoping to get someone's attention. He begins to get very cold. He fumbles with his key and tries in vain to get the door to open, while the man inside, warm in his wool overcoat and fur cap, gestures and yells at the glass. The man who is freezing yells back. I strain to hear what is being said but to no avail. I am in a hotel room across the street. The warm man inside abruptly turns his back and walks out of my view, causing another round of animated shouting and banging from outside. I grab my camera and focus in on the scene, sensing something bad is about to happen; I can feel it. I can see small droplets of water freezing to the face of that man outside the glass door. I wonder why none of the people walking by will stop and help and just at that moment, it happens. The man inside puts a piece of paper to the glass. I focus in my 300 mm lens and read: "I'm sorry, sir, the locks are frozen and we can't get them open. Look up, your wife is dropping your heavy coat out of the window." And with that, everything changed—a terrible situation turned good. Salvation fell from the hands of a woman five stories above. As the woman slammed the window, he caught the coat and greedily put it on over his jogging attire and then began a molasses-slow trot to the coffee house a block down the street.

Notice how fulfilling the completion of the story was, how you had to keep reading to know what happened, and how good it felt to reach the conclusion. You already drew some conclusions about how it would end, and I gave you just enough information to fill in the blanks at the right time so you could draw the correct conclusions. That is exactly what happens when you tell a story to a prospect or to anyone you want to deeply persuade.

Stories have inherent power. We have learned from stories

our whole lives. We have learned to listen to stories and look for the moral or the meaning of the story. We have also learned that stories are engaging. We have a different way of listening to a story than we do to facts and figures; in fact, you can feel the difference in your body and see it in your posture.

If someone tells us a story, we are drawn in and we listen to it. We find ourselves drawn deeply if they are a good storyteller. If they are a poor storyteller, we still excuse that in many cases and try to make the story work for us.

Stories become very powerful when you are persuading people.

The challenge that many people have when they are persuading is that they do not take the time to think about what their story is. They throw out a number of facts or they throw out a number of ideas. They just do it in a kind of litany or a bullet-pointed way and that really is not a story. It is more like a story problem that we have to solve. I don't know if you are like me, but I love stories and hate story problems!

When you just give facts and figures it forces people to go into a linear, logical kind of evaluation process: "Does $1+1=2$?" If the answer is no, then this is not relevant, or valid, or even credible to me. The result is that they begin to become skeptical and start trying to find reasons you are wrong instead of going deeper with you.

If you want to fly under your customer's radar or that of the people you are trying to persuade, then it is important that you tell a well-crafted story. Your story should be full of imagery and use powerful verbs to move the reader or listener. There is a big difference between a green sofa and an overstuffed chair with arms that come up to your ears when you sink into it with a child on your lap. There is an even bigger difference between an

Internet Service Provider and the one place on the Internet where you can learn and connect and become. It is your old-fashioned library meets the movie *The Matrix*. Your stories need to create connections between what the person is thinking, what he already believes, and what you want him to believe and do.

Stories are very persuasive for many reasons and on many levels. We are used to listening to stories; it is how we are taught from the very earliest age. Oral traditions were passed on by word of mouth before print or electronic communications were readily accessible and for many continue today in the form of family biographies. We have also learned that when someone tells a story, we should listen no matter how badly told the story is. At a very young age you discovered that stories carry messages and you learned how to decipher them, but that deciphering required your attention (as persuaders, we want our listener's attention). Stories are also persuasive because they put the listener into the action. Whether written, oral, or delivered electronically, good stories put us in a kind of trance: We see ourselves as part of the action and you can take no action external to your body until you have first taken it in your mind. You must imagine it first to make it happen. Stories engage both hemispheres of the brain; they encourage you to remember and to feel. Stories engage the emotions.

Whenever you set out to persuade you must think about what you want to say, the message you want to get across, and what it is that you want the person to do. Then you begin to craft your story.

Persuasive stories are different from regular stories fundamentally because they are designed to get your attention, develop a high level of interest, create desire, and allow you to draw the conclusions necessary to take the action I want you to take. One of the not-so-obvious powers of a well-told persuasive story is that no one else can tell the story the way you do, especially your competition. It is not surprising that the description I just gave you sounds a lot like the AIDA (Attention, Interest, Desire, Action) formula that has been the staple of advertising for the better part of a century. The reason is simple: The best advertising people are phenomenal storytellers. They just broke storytelling down to its simplest and purest form as it related to advertising.

There is an important distinction to make between persuasive stories and storybook stories. While storybook stories share many of the same structure and delivery elements as persuasive stories, they vary in their intent and purpose. Storybook stories have the intent and purpose of entertaining the reader; they are designed to affect you and satisfy your need for a form of escapism. Persuasive stories take advantage of the proven elements of novels and other forms of oral storytelling, but they are designed to create a different outcome. They are designed to get you to come to a predetermined conclusion and take a predetermined course of action designed by the persuader.

HOW TO TELL A PERSUASIVE STORY

Some people can tell a great story every time and others simply cannot get it right no matter how hard they try. But storytelling is a skill that we can all perfect and use at will. Here are the steps to a persuasive story:

1. *Know your story.* The reason most of the stories you tell right now are not persuasive is that they have not been well thought out or the material and experience are not your own.

You have pieces that you can bring to mind or a specific example, but there is no real flow to the pieces so it feels more like you are rattling off bullet points or dropping pieces in. Worse, you are told stories by other people that you are supposed to adapt to be your own and you don't have all of the background information to make the story authentic and complete. The most persuasive stories are those with which you have some firsthand experience.

For stories to be well received you must know what the listener or reader needs to hear in order to have his needs fulfilled. I want you to think of something you sell or something you must persuade someone of regularly. In order for a story to be persuasive, you must begin by outlining what you have. What are the points that must be made every time you talk to someone in order for him to be persuaded? What are the things that your audience must know or will have questions about that you must answer for them to be fulfilled? What will they get out of your suggested solution? List all of those elements on a piece of paper.

Next, layer on your proof. What testimonials and proof do you have that will convince me what you are saying is true? Who else is doing what you are asking me to do? List your elements of proof on your paper now.

Now, make me emotional. What is the pain I will feel, or other people may have felt, from not buying what you are selling? Did they lose money or respect? Did they suffer a loss of some kind? Are they setting themselves up for some kind of failure? What is it that will happen or might happen if they don't take action? List that now.

Set me up for the questions I should ask or will most certainly ask. Identify those questions and their answers and write them down on your list as well.

Finally, what do you want me to do? Write this down very specifically, as well as the steps I will need to take in order to do it. Also write down what my objections will be: If I need to get financing, put that down; or if I must get approval from the board, write that down. Get all the objections out of the way.

2. *Lay out your story.* A persuasive story answers the questions of *who, what, when, where, why,* and *how* in the following format:

A. *Grab me by the ears.* In a moment I will show you how to develop a grab-me-by-the-ears statement. But for now, know that you must command attention. You want a statement so powerful that people 15 feet away will stop what they are doing to come and listen or they will strain their ears and good manners to eavesdrop.

B. *Lay the foundation.* In this section of your story you lay the groundwork. You include any information I must know to understand the story, fill in the holes in my knowledge, and give me enough background that I can understand what you are saying. In this section you insert the things that the person must know that you identified on paper earlier.

C. *Engage my emotions.* Get me excited or move me into a place where I am experiencing pain, lust, desire, or loss. Grab at least three points from the list you created that are emotional and put those in this section of your story. Be sure you use points that I am going to have a hard time disagreeing with or that I know immediately will happen to me or have happened to someone I know. (If I cannot relate here, then it is time to lay in a story about someone like me, describing what happened to them.)

D. *Layer on the proof.* Give me an example featuring someone I know, preferably, or again, someone just like me. Tell me his story, letting me know that this is a real person. If you have no other reference, tell a story about yourself that adds credibility and proof at this point.

E. *Answer my questions.* Lay out at least three to five of the questions I will most likely have and answer them preemptively. Let me know that you are an expert because you know exactly what it is that I have questions about. Layer on more proof here, showing how someone else had that exact question answered and what the outcome was.

F. *Give me enough information that I can draw your conclusion.* Give me only enough detail so that I have a few small questions left that require an interaction. Tell me what I have to do, by when, and why I should. In psychological terms this causes us to do a transderivational search to try and find answers and meaning.

G. *Get my feedback.* I want to know that I got the point; I don't want to have to guess, so ask. Allow me to give you more information now that I have heard your story. Let me demonstrate how what you have just said applies to me.

That is how a persuasive story is laid out. Once you have laid out the story in this format, you can begin adding in the part that makes the story interesting. You must lay out every story you intend to use to persuade in just this format to ensure your success. Whether you are telling the story one-on-one or one-to-many, or telling the story in writing, in an ad, or on the Internet, the format remains the same because ultimately the best stories are told to one person at a time, no matter how many people are in the audience or how they receive your message. Persuasive stories engage you individually and they bring you along through the process because they are laid out in a way that pulls you in and hooks you and everyone else who is reading or listening.

3. *Tell your story.* Telling your story is the fun part and the part where most people fail. Think back to when you were a child and someone read to you (if you can't remember, go to a library or bookstore where they read to children and watch). It was completely enthralling when someone read a story to you, but there was always one person who you really wanted to read you the story. That person was the one who made the story come to life. Dragons roared through the reader, causing you to squeal in terror; maidens talked in high squeaky voices that tickled the insides of your ears; woodcutters' deep voices could rattle your bones. You were spellbound and you couldn't wait for the very next word. When your favorite reader was reading, you couldn't hear enough stories. Persuasive storytellers engage your senses with their body language, with their tone, with their eye contact, and with their emotions. They transfix you with emotion, tickle you with humor, and lead you to the only logical conclusion anyone could make. And, oh, what a feeling it is.

When you first begin telling your story you must grab your listeners or readers by the ears. The best way to grab them by the ears is to have an interesting hook. Sometimes it can be as simple as saying, "Let me tell you a story." Or, you can start out with "You know, I just thought of . . . ," or with a question: "Has this ever happened to you?" Any question will lead people easily into a state where they will listen to your story.

If you ask a question, most people feel compelled to answer. That gives you permission to begin the story. A great way to deliver a question is to ask, "Have you ever experienced . . . ?" So, if I ask you this question, "Have you ever experienced a time where money was so tight that you couldn't imagine spending a dime, and yet you knew, positively, that the best thing you could do for your future was to invest every dime you had?", you are forced to go inside yourself to try to find a matching experience. (Do it now, noticing how hard you are willing to search for a matching answer.) People will always find an experience like that in their lives, even if they did not take the action they felt they should have taken. They have the actual experience and emotional experience to connect with the story and they will find them. Once they have acknowledged that they have or have not had the experience, it gives you a chance to move right into a story. You need only alter your story slightly to engage people who have not had the experience by telling them the story of your own experience.

Allow me to demonstrate a few additional secrets of storytelling, as I tell you a selling story.

The very best way to tell stories is to tell them in chunks. So, you start out with your question, or whatever is going to hook your audience. Then, you think about the different kinds of people that you will be talking to on a regular basis. Most of us only talk to four or five different kinds of people throughout a typical engagement in our business.

There are buyers. There are people who are skeptical. There are people who have questions. You are going to have a different piece or a slightly different story that you tell each of those people. Those links are the pieces of your story that link it to any buyer or person that you need to persuade. We want to start the story, hook him in, and then we want to link it to something that's important and powerful to him.

Here is an example of how I would do that if I were selling cars. "You're here for the red car, right?" I might simply ask, or "What's important in a car to you?", or "What's important about a car for you?" Here's another good question: "What's important about this car to you?" I would get the person to give me additional information, then, beginning with the answer, here's how the conversation would go.

"Well, I'm really looking for a red car because I'd like a sports car. But I want it to be a convertible and I want it to be fast, and I like those new low-profile tires."

"You know, I just remembered this, there is a guy who came in here a couple of days ago who does parking lot races. You know those races where they have cones in the parking lot and you get to race through them? He really liked red cars, too. But you know what he told me? He said when he was racing that a dark car actually served him better because people could spot it on the track easier in the midst of all the red cars, and he wanted all eyes on him.

"Everybody who has a sports car seems to want it red or bright blue or something like that. So instead, he chose a black car because it stood out and for him that really worked. Now, I am not saying that is right for you, of course. But, if you like to be unique, and you really like the look of these low-profile tires, and speed is important to you, then it is something to consider.

"Is standing out from the crowd important to you, or do you want a car that matches a lot of others on the street?" Here you get another piece of information from the buyer, who gives it willingly; he's become a part of your story. "No, no, standing out in the crowd is important to me too." "Okay, then maybe we could look at these two cars."

If you had a red car, could you have sold it to him? Sure. But what if you really wanted to serve the guy better? Maybe a black car would help him be more unique in his look, or maybe you didn't have a red car with all the options he wanted. Maybe the black car had more margin for you. You shifted his wants through telling a simple story about what happened with someone else and linking it together with his criteria.

Finally, the end of your story comes—and we try to make these stories very simple—it is simply a close. What is the point of the story? What was the purpose of the story? If you have told the story correctly, the answer is clearly, "This is the right choice for me." The result of hearing the purpose of the story should get you to draw a logical conclusion to take action. That is what you are really trying to do.

In the case of the car, you are trying to move the prospect from a red car to a black car. So, the purpose of the story is saying, "Listen, if you want to be different, if you want to set yourself apart, then you buy a black car because everyone else is in a sea of red and yours is the only black car. That is the one that gets you noticed." It begins to shift his criteria. It begins to move him forward in a way that nothing else could.

WRITING PERSUASIVELY MEANS WRITING DOWN GOOD STORIES

Telling your story in writing is very similar. If you want to make your sales letters more powerful, write in stories. When you are writing—and this is very important—stories become very powerful in breaking up the copy that you are using. If you want to move people to action, you need to have something that keeps rehooking them and getting them to read on and on. Everyone has probably heard the purpose of a headline. The purpose of a headline is to get you to read the first sentence. And, the purpose of the first sentence is to get you to read the next, and so on.

Stories do that because people begin to look for the next piece of the story, the next part of the puzzle. Some of you outside of the United States may never have heard of Paul Harvey, but Paul Harvey tells stories. All he does is tell stories on the radio and he has been doing it for decades and people still tune in with great anticipation, especially since there is a good chance they have already heard the story, but not the way he tells it. He tells half the story, he goes to a commercial break, and then he comes back and says, "And now for the rest of the story." People cannot change the station. Unless they were completely uninterested in the story in the first place, people cannot turn the dial during the commercial break because they don't want to miss the rest of the story. Harvey created a cult of listeners with his persuasive stories, told so well that you *cannot* not stay around and listen.

When you write good letters or ads, you simply tell good stories. You can leave the story off anywhere and keep the readers coming back for more, just like Paul Harvey. You can tell three-quarters of the story or half the story. Then, you say, "You know, I'm going to get to the rest of the story in just a second, but here are a couple of things that I think are important to note." Then, you begin setting your criteria for what it is that you want them to buy by linking the story to what you are selling.

Then, you tell another piece of the story. You link it together. Finally, at the end, when they have had to read through this whole letter to get to the end of the story, you have now given them all of the information they need to make the only logical conclusion they can, which is to buy from you.

As you craft your stories, be sure you are crafting them in pieces that can be linked to each part of your buying process, as well as linked to each kind of person that might be reading your letter, walking in to talk to you, on the phone with you, or listening to you as you are being interviewed in the media.

TELLING YOUR STORY TO THE MEDIA

Everyone wonders how to get their story into the media. The best answer is that you have an opportunity to really hook any reporter by telling her a great story. What is a reporter's real purpose? People miss this. The biggest public relations companies in the nation miss this simple key. The purpose of reporters is to tell a story. That's the only thing that they do and they're always looking for stories to tell.

As I did research for this book, I used a service called Profnet to query public relations firms about questions I had or people I wanted to interview. Within moments of sending out my query, I began to get responses, nearly all of them flat. The media releases I received were full of hyperbole and promises and rarely paid off in terms of the experts they described. Most I immediately discarded. But the ones that I kept, the ones that really got my attention, were those that actually involved me emotionally. They pulled me in with a compelling story and made me yearn to know more. Out of over a hundred responses that I got for one section of this book, I interviewed one person, and it was a person who wrote me an e-mail so compelling I could not get to the phone to call her quickly enough. All the other responses went into the trash. Interestingly enough, I was also able to tell something about the people I would be interviewing by the story or lack of story that they told when they sent me their initial response. Those who were lucid, good storytellers were the best interviews with the best information. The rest ultimately did not end up in the book.

So, if you can give reporters something that they want, in a format they're used to—a story—who do you think they are going to listen to? You, or somebody who wrote a very benign headline on a flaccid media release that doesn't really draw anybody in, or promise anything, or get them emotionally engaged?

Again, the power of stories is their ability to emotionally engage people. It grabs people by the brain and it grabs people by the heart. It slams the two of them together so that they can listen as one. The result is that reporters are moved by the stories you tell.

PRACTICE YOUR STORYTELLING

In order to be a good storyteller you must practice your story and polish your delivery. Just tell the story once out loud to yourself and then continue to work on improving it from there. One of the best investments you can make when you are learning to tell stories is a cheap microphone that you can record into your PC with. Tell the story into your microphone. Listen to what you are trying to say. Is it coming across appropriately? Do you sound authentic? Do you sound convincing? Do you sound emotional in the right places?

Here is the other thing about stories. If you tell stories without any inflection, without any emotion in your voice, they do not work as well. If you write stories without any inflection or any emotion, they do not work at all.

Imagine if I told you the story of "The Three Little Pigs" or "Red Riding Hood" and just spoke in a monotone voice. Go ahead and read this in your head in your best imitation of my monotone delivery: "The first pig made his house of straw and the wolf came and blew it down. The second pig made his house of sticks. Sticks are not good construction material when they're set against a wolf with powerful lungs. So, the wolf came and blew them down." When looking at the story in this writing, it doesn't move you at all. But when you read the original . . . well, you get the picture.

When you tell stilted stories, people immediately disconnect with you. They are trying to figure out "How do I make this interesting for me?" So, listen to what you are saying and read what you are writing. Make sure that you are using good examples. Make sure that you are using good and powerful verbs that draw people in, that get people to take action, that get them to see things you want them to see in their minds and get them to do the things you want them to do.

One of the things I do on a regular basis is look at pictures and describe what is going on in the picture. It doesn't even have to be the right story for the picture. I just make up stories about the picture and describe what is happening in the scene. Then, I show the picture to someone and I say, "Let me tell you the story of this picture."

If they look at that and say, "Wow, that's really interesting," then I know I did a good job of describing it. If they say, "Really, that's what's happening," or they do not respond at all, then I know I probably did not do a very good job of describing it.

This process is just a way of beginning to learn how to tell a story, to learn how to create a story of your own, to learn how to pull people in, to be able to take situations that are foreign to you right now and be able to easily and quickly put a story together around it, because that is what is required of you when you set out to persuade.

There are three stories everyone one should have at the ready. Your personal story is the first. When people want to know more about you, you need to tell them a compelling, interesting minibiography appropriate to your situation. Like all stories, the minibiography is built in chunks so that you can add more pieces when necessary and appropriate. The second story is the story of your company, and the third is the story of your product or service. Learn to tell your story well and you will quickly improve your ability to persuade far beyond that of your peers or competition.

 Chapter Review

☞ Stories slide past our logic and engage emotion.

☞ Stories are persuasive because we have been trained from our earliest childhood to listen to and enjoy stories.

☞ Stories allow you to put the person you are persuading into the picture; they get to be a part of the action.

☞ Stories are comfortable because they are delivered in a familiar format. Your stories need to be laid out in the proper format to achieve maximum impact.

☞ Your stories must be designed to heighten emotional awareness of the problem your solution is solving.

☞ When you put your story together be sure that you employ all six of Rudyard Kipling's honest serving-men in developing your story. Answer the questions of what, why, when, how, where, and who.

☞ Successful stories shift the criteria of the person you are persuading.

(Continued)

Success Questions

☞ What is my story today and how can I make it better?

☞ What stories do I know that I have not told that would add power to my position?

☞ What testimonials do I have that I can turn into powerful persuasion stories or that I can layer into my stories?

☞ What are the five most important things I have learned in this chapter that I need to apply to become more persuasive?

☞ Whose stories do I enjoy listening to most and what can I take away from those presentations that will make my own stories more powerful?

6

GURUDOM

When men destroy their old gods they will find new ones to take their place.

— Pearl S. Buck

Leaders don't force people to follow—they invite them on a journey.

— Charles S. Lauer

Persuasion becomes much easier when you are a recognized expert because people are looking for someone credible in whom they can trust and believe. They are much more willing to open their minds to new possibilities. Once you develop your status as an expert it is easy to begin to develop a following and people who follow you are much easier to convince than those who do not know you at all.

Think of the gurus we look to for advice daily. Dr. Phil McGraw is the undisputed king of self-help and psychology. Rush Limbaugh is the guru of all things conservative. Peter Drucker is the most lauded leader of the organizational and management movement. Every one of these people has something in common: They have a following, people who willingly listen to them, who believe in them, and who lend their credibility to them each time they recommend them to their friends or colleagues.

When I talk about gurudom, I use the term as one that encompasses everything from being a simple expert in a field or subject to holding sway over large groups of people. For the purposes of persuasion it encompasses the first two definitions of the word: the first, a personal spiritual teacher related to Hinduism and Tibetan Buddhism, and the second and most common usage for our purposes, a trusted counselor and advisor; a mentor (*American Heritage Dictionary of the English Language*, 4th Ed.).

It is important that everyone who persuades professionally or who hopes simply to negotiate better deals becomes an expert, and hopefully a well-recognized expert, in his or her field. Over the next few pages, we will explore how you can develop your particular skills and beliefs into recognized expert status (if you follow the plan all the way through, maybe even celebrity expert status).

I want you to think about your own experience for a moment. You have probably purchased something in the past you needed but were not well qualified to buy, which for many of us is some technology product. Depending on the big box store you chose the experience probably went a little like this: You go in and shop, you read the tags, you push the buttons, you look at all the products in that category. You dismiss several salespeople along the way because you want to look a little before you buy. Then, the time comes; you have narrowed your selection down to a couple of systems based on what you have seen. You motion for the salesperson who gladly comes to your assistance. You ask the difference between the two products and look forward to a thoughtful explanation. Then it comes. The salesperson reads to you the descriptions of the product from the tags on the machines that you have already scrutinized. You ask what that means and they cannot explain it. They have completely destroyed their credibility and the likelihood of you buying anything at that point is very low.

Contrast that experience to this one. You walk into the store and begin looking at MP3 players. The salesperson walks up and asks if this will be your first MP3 player. You answer yes. The salesperson says, "I've had seven of them. In addition to this job, I'm a disc jockey for parties and weddings so I'm always trying to find the best one I can so I do not have to drag CDs everywhere. The hard part for me is finding one that has high enough sound quality, a large enough storage capacity, and that is reasonably priced. What will you be using yours for?" You explain that you travel a lot and want something that will help you fend off people who like to talk to you the whole flight, interrupting your work time. The salesperson goes on with his explanation. "If you do not mind, I think I can help you narrow it down to these two choices, let me explain why. First, unless you are like me and need to have five to ten thousand songs on your MP3 player at all times, there is no reason to buy one with a giant hard drive. And, if you are not going to be using it to hold photos or watch movies, which are very time consuming to load, then you do not need a color display. Both of these units will hold about three thousand songs, that is, about two hundred CDs' worth of music, and cost less than two hundred and fifty dollars. I really like the sound quality of both of these, too. I do not think you'll be able to tell the difference between the MP3 and what you hear on your CD player. I know I cannot and my clients have never said anything about the quality when I've played it for them at their parties. This is the one I think you should buy, it is twenty dollars more but the accessories are much less expensive so you'll save money in the long run."

The difference is that you walk out of the second store with your new technology purchase and, assuming that your product delivers on the promise, a trusted ally when buying personal electronics. That example simply shows how demonstrating an area of expertise (in this case the salesperson was also a disc jockey) keeps the customer from questioning the salesperson's recommendation, because of the salesperson's perceived expertise and product knowledge.

Now imagine you are trying to convince your customer to use your business over your much larger competitor. Your competitor makes a reasonably convincing argument, so you go to work. You demonstrate your expert knowledge by giving a very detailed overview of the client's problem and possible solutions. You layer on the case studies showing how you have helped similar companies solve similar problems. Then you bring out your big guns. You provide the prospective client with a copy of your book demonstrating your knowledge in the area and direct him to two major trade magazines with current articles about your particular methodology. Finally, you suggest he learn more about you, by watching the DVD showing your numerous interviews on CNN, MSNBC, and Fox News.

Suddenly your value goes up. There is significant reason to immediately trust that you will be able to give him a better solution, even if it costs a little more. Each one of the media outlets that interviewed you gave you third-party credibility. Your case study further deepened that credibility and your book demonstrated that you clearly have more-than-average knowledge about the problem he faces and the solution required.

You are well on your way to reaching the enviable heights of gurudom. The final level is to create a personal experience for each of your clients that is perfect. You deliver on your promises, you show them that their decision and faith was well placed, and you deepen the relationship. The result is you create a follower, someone who is willing to support you and always choose you without question. At this point, it takes a major intervention to pry him away from you. He has a new set of beliefs and a new schema through which he views providers of your product, service, or ideas.

Being a guru also does something else for you—it allows you to be discovered in ways that would have otherwise eluded you. When people do a search for your name, company name, or category on Google, they find multiple references for you in media outlets where you have been interviewed, giving you more desirability. They find your blog (a blog is literally a web log, an online diary that is rapidly creating a place in journalism as a legitimate media outlet) and read your most current posts on your area of expertise. They easily found your blog because search engines currently rank blog pages very high in terms of relevancy to search terms. You are also discovered when your peers reference you in interviews and on television shows, and your book opens doors that you never could before you were published.

By now I am confident you are convinced of what developing your own guru status can do for you. The important thing to know about this whole process is that no matter how small your business currently is or how small your audience is, becoming the foremost expert in your area of influence is the single smartest thing you can do.

HOW TO BECOME A RECOGNIZED EXPERT IN THIRTY DAYS

No matter how widely you are or are not known today, within 30 days virtually anyone can be well on the way to becoming a well-recognized expert. The process is really relatively simple, but it does require a focused effort on your part to ensure your plan remains on track. You must maintain the effort as well. Gurus come and go very quickly—the ones who last are the ones who focus on maintaining their relevance and visibility.

Being relevant is the single most important key to being a well-recognized guru. You must be sure that your knowledge is current and that the information you can provide can solve problems or present new ideas quickly, concisely, and with a certain amount of personal flair (review Chapter 3 on persona). Finally, develop opinions. They can be similar to others in your field or dissenting. One thing all gurus have in common is opinions they can call their own.

Here is the roadmap for success to become a recognized expert in 30 days:

1. Determine your area of expertise.

   ☛ Clearly define a specific area where you are already knowledgeable. Decide on what subject you want to become an expert.

2. Thoroughly study your subject matter.

   ☛ Many experts agree that it takes about 1,000 hours of practice to become an expert at something: language, an instrument, or any other activity you want to perform expertly.

☞ Make a spreadsheet with 1,000 blocks in it. Write down each time you spend one hour on developing your expertise. And, write down what you studied, learned, proved, or applied.

3. Begin to develop opinions.

☞ Experts have opinions and share them.
☞ Begin writing essays, articles, and papers.
☞ Spend time sharing your opinions with reporters and other influence professionals who can spread your word.
☞ Begin speaking publicly in appropriate forums about your expertise.

4. Share your opinions and original ideas.

☞ Give talks, ideally at trade organizations; even small groups like Toastmasters give you the opportunity to begin documenting your expertise. This is not a time to worry about being paid for your knowledge and opinions; it is a time to cement your status as a guru.
☞ Get testimonials from those groups about your expertise and your ability to succinctly share the expertise.

5. Write a book, an article, or a white paper; create an audio book.

☞ A book gives you instant credibility.
☞ The book does not have to be long.
☞ It is a living document that demonstrates to everyone your expert status and it gives you, and potentially your company, a legacy.
☞ Create an audio book; they are fast and inexpensive to produce if you are going to self-publish.

6. Get your own radio program.
7. Write a blog.
8. Promote yourself.

I want to explore each of the points above in more detail so you can have all of the information necessary to put each one of these points to work for you. Virtually anyone can do each of the items listed above. The next few paragraphs demonstrate the simplest ways to make each step a reality.

Determine Your Area of Expertise

Focus is crucial to rapid learning. Determining your area of expertise is the very first step to becoming an expert. Generalizations are not enough. When I set out to study persuasion I did not do it with the purpose of becoming the foremost expert in the area of persuasion. But over time as I became better known in the sales and marketing arena, I knew I needed to set myself apart, to be different from everyone around me. I decided to leverage my current research to become an expert on persuading people. Once you decide what it is you want to be known for, where your area of expertise can lie, then you can set out to carve your place in gurudom. You must have a good basis of knowledge in your industry and by limiting your focus you can become much more knowledgeable.

Thoroughly Study Your Subject Matter

In order to be an expert you need to thoroughly understand your subject matter. Get additional training or knowledge when you do not understand something fully or when the matter is outside your current realm of knowledge. Be sure you study the current thinking of the key thought leaders in your industry, and if possible learn from them directly to deepen your knowledge and speed your assimilation.

Begin to Develop Opinions

As mentioned earlier, experts have opinions. You must have opinions as well if you hope to persuade and be recognized as a thought leader. If you do not have an original opinion, then study the opinions of the thought leaders and build on those. If you strongly agree, develop an opinion about why they are right, and if you do not agree, develop an opinion about why they are wrong. Ideally, you will develop original ideas and opinions, as those are the most valuable to your followers and to those who would spread your message, including the media. Once you have developed your opinions and original ideas, package them into useable sound bites so that you can quickly and clearly demonstrate your opinion and why it is correct and valuable to those who hear it.

Share Your Opinions and Original Ideas

It is important at this stage to share your ideas and opinions. You need to see the fruits of all your hard work. Establishing yourself is the first step to developing a following. Be sure the people who you ultimately wish to influence are made aware of your opinions and ideas.

This is the time to begin approaching the media that serves your industry. Identify appropriate trade or consumer magazines that serve your market and open a dialog with the editors about your topic. Nearly every magazine has an editorial calendar, the description of what stories will appear in upcoming issues, listed on its web site. Use the editorial calendar as a starting point for developing your relationship. It is important you identify why you are a good fit for the article and a credible expert and be able to deliver that message clearly and succinctly, as you will have a very short audience with the editor when you connect.

There are also services you can purchase that give you the opportunity to receive active leads from editors looking for people to interview on virtually any topic. The best of these services is PR NEWSWIRE (www.prnewswire.com). You can receive feeds several times a day from dozens of editors looking for experts just like you to interview for stories that will typically appear very soon.

Write a Book, an Article, or a White Paper; Create an Audio Book

Imposing as it sounds to some, writing a book and getting it into print is easier now than ever. Following the traditional route of identifying a large publisher and having your book published remains the preferred outlet for your book. I am not going to attempt to show you how to go through the process of developing a proposal and contacting editors, but there are many very good books available on the subject and a small investment can be invaluable.

For many people self-publishing is a very acceptable way to get your book into print. Self-published books are beginning to receive much more positive attention; when it is purchased on Amazon.com, very few people will know the difference if the book is well produced. There are many companies that will help you through the process of self-publishing a book, and print on demand makes the cost very affordable as you can purchase minimal numbers of copies.

Later I describe a method by which you can write a book, article, or white paper in 30 days or less, but first I want to talk about articles and white papers. Nearly all magazines are looking for well-written, timely articles, particularly trade magazines. Again, in the beginning and maybe forever, the idea is not to turn your writing into a profit center. Many people who write as a regular part of their efforts to persuade will tell you that you do not make money from a book or article; you make money because of the book or article.

Articles that are well written and incorporate your unique ideas and opinions are great ways to develop your following and to give credibility to your positions. Most people believe articles are only written by well-qualified journalists or experts. While that is true, it is also true that people reading the articles typically give them credence simply because of their belief that if it is printed it is better than the information they themselves possess.

White papers are detailed reports that explain ideas, theories, or processes in a way that incorporates your ideas and opinions to deliver a convincing message about why some idea is correct or true. White papers are valuable in building your credibility as a guru because they offer people a detailed look inside your company and into your thought process.

White papers do not have to be written by you and they do not have to contain information that is yours alone. You can borrow from research (keeping in mind all copyright and legal restrictions) and even have your ideas researched and developed (and written) by others. Ghostwriting of white papers is frequent and well accepted. If you do nothing else to develop your guru status, write your first white paper today and circulate it among your peers and those you wish to influence.

The biggest reason that most people do not complete this step is that they feel writing is too overwhelming and make the process too difficult. Let me share a very simple process that anyone can use to develop a book, article, or white paper in 30 days or less.

☞ Decide on a topic (notice I said *topic*, not *title*). Too many people get caught up in writing the perfect title and never get past it.

☞ Write out your table of contents or overview of the article, one idea or chapter to a page.

☞ List seven points you want to make in each chapter on the table of contents page; alternatively, list the seven points you want to make, one to a page, if you are writing an article.

☞ Put each of those table of contents pages or each of the seven points pages in a separate folder.

☞ Collect any needed research, facts, quotes, photos, or other material for each topic in your table of contents or seven points pages and put them in the folder. Initial collection needs to be done in one day per topic or less. (Here is a hint: If you really get busy, you can typically put it all together in a day or two, tops, if you are focused only on that task.)

☞ Begin writing your book. Start by filling in the information around your seven points in each chapter or build your article around the seven points. Write until you have completed all the necessary information for the seven points. Optionally, go to the next chapter or stop for the day. Be sure that as you write you answer the questions of *who, what, when, where, why*, and *how*. If you are uncomfortable writing, find a co-author or hire someone to write for you. It truly is that simple.

☛ Continue the process until you are done with all of your chapters.

☛ Congratulate yourself on having written your very first book, article, or white paper.

The very same process applies to an audio book with one exception: Once you have written everything down, you (or the voice talent you hire) go to the recording studio and record your book onto a CD. You can also record white papers and place them on your web site for people you hope to persuade.

Get Your Own Radio Program

Getting on the radio works very well for establishing credibility and virtually anyone can do it today. Nearly every AM radio station has blocks of time they sell to people like you and me for their own radio programs. The blocks typically range from 30 to 60 minutes. As of this writing, you can have your own radio program for as little as $60 per week.

The nice thing about radio is that you do not have to do it in your hometown (it is beneficial if that is your primary area of influence), since you can do radio over the phone from anywhere. You simply call up and they run your program live or you prerecord it and they run it in the timeslot you own.

Many successful people have developed radio programs this way and go on to syndication; some do it themselves and others hire syndication companies to do it for them. Depending on your purpose and desired reach, as well as the effort you are willing to put into the project, syndication can make sense. Often, for the sake of time, buying more stations makes sense as well.

Here is a little-known secret of radio programming. The minute you have your own program you are an official media personality with all the privileges that brings, which for our purposes means access. There are very few people or PR departments that will turn down an opportunity to be on the air if there is an obvious fit between what you are talking about and the person you wish to interview. Remember earlier when we were talking about being known by the company you keep? Well, this is your key to the city, so to speak. Plus, the moment you interview someone and help her spread her message or build her credibility, she becomes indebted to you and is very likely to return this favor if she can.

I do not want to leave you with the idea that just because you have a radio program it gives you instant access to anyone in commerce or industry. It does not; the higher the profile of the person you hope to interview, the harder the interview is to get. Use your influence with the people you are interviewing. Ask if they can introduce you to others you want to interview when they have the connection. For most people who are building a following, interviewing the very best-known people in the industry is not really their goal, as there are dozens if not hundreds of lesser-known experts to give you and your show credibility. Remember that the purpose of your show is to build your status as a guru, not to build your status as a radio interviewer.

Write a Blog

The great thing about writing a web log is that no one expects the ideas to be long like an article or a book, but no one minds if they are, if they are well written.

Blogs are wonderful tools for a number of reasons. The first is that they give you a place to practice your opinions. That does not mean that they cannot be well thought out, but blogs by their nature have a limited readership, though often very dedicated. Once you have put your idea out in a blog, you will often get immediate feedback both from people who send you e-mails, directly sharing their thoughts and ideas, and from those who link to your blog posts in their own. As your blog and your ideas gain more traction, many other bloggers will often put you on their recommended reading lists so people reading their blogs will read yours too. These bloggers have a lot of credibility with their readers and they willingly transfer it to you.

The second reason that blogs are such powerful tools is that they are treated very favorably by the search engines. Because of their keyword search relevancy and their frequent update they tend to show up much higher in search engine results. Let us use my own blog as an example. Many of the search terms for which I would have to pay large sums of money every time someone clicked on them in Google or other paid placement search engines are included in the posts that I make, and the result is that my blog ends up in the top position among all of the search engines that I want.

When writing your blog, the important research to do ahead of time is the keywords and search phrases that people search to find you and your category. There are great places to do research to find out how many people search particular terms or phrases, but none better than http://inventory.overture.com. Simply type your word or phrase in the search box and it will immediately let you know how many people are searching for that word or term and what else they are searching that is related. Once you have determined what terms and phrases people use, you simply begin to create blog posts around those terms and phrases. Here is a little-known secret: Including those in the headline of the posting also helps with search engine positioning and they are often the first thing people searching for your term see, which encourages them to click through because it is very relevant.

For best results keep your blog posts between 200 and 400 words. That makes them rank higher in the search engine results. Also be sure to create links out of your blog to web sites of companies or people that you mention—that also gives you a higher ranking. It also lets those people find out about you if they do not already know you. Everyone checks his or her own name in a search engine; if they do not, they should and probably will soon.

Post to your blog two or three times a week and keep the ideas fresh and flowing. If you do not have anything original you can talk about, talk about current industry trends or comment on particular ideas others are circulating.

Promote Yourself

Gurus become gurus because they are not afraid to spread their own gospel and you should not be afraid either. You simply have to think about building your guru status as a necessary part of doing business. The best-known typically win the long race and you are building your foundation now.

Be sure that all your press clippings get up on your web site where others can see them. Share your successes by sending out appropriate articles to your clients or prospects that you write. Think of them as additional marketing opportunities. The responsibility for spreading your message is your own but the better job you do, the quicker your newfound following will start spreading it for you.

Take full advantage of the opportunity that your newfound

gurudom will present for you and the doors it will open. Focus your efforts on spreading your ideas and message at every appropriate opportunity and share your successes at getting your message heard with those clients closest to you. The result will be that you become a leader in your industry, someone with whom people want to do business. The only thing that defines a leader is the number and quality of followers he or she has.

Gurudom is yours for the taking. What will you do to enhance your followers' experiences today?

Chapter Review

☛ People want to listen to and believe those people who have apparent knowledge they themselves do not possess. They want to learn from those they perceive as having specialized knowledge that can be beneficial.

☛ Creating guru status is not really difficult but it takes a concentrated effort.

☛ Gurus and experts have opinions they openly share, some agreeing with industry norms, others not. Often the best-known experts challenge norms. Develop your opinions and share them today.

☛ Once you have developed your status, your followers will spread your message for you.

☛ Write a book, a white paper, an article, or a blog, and use the power of the press to give your ideas more credibility and weight.

(Continued)

Success Questions

☛ In what specific area of my industry am I already an expert or do I want to be an expert?

☛ What do I need to study or learn in order to round out my experience as an expert?

☛ What have I done already that gives me some standing as a recognized expert?

☛ What is the first book, white paper, or article I will write and to whom will I give it?

☛ Who are the people currently willing to look to me as a thought leader and how can I influence them to share their beliefs with others like them?

7

DESIRE TO BELIEVE

What a man believes upon grossly insufficient evidence is an index into his desires—desires of which he himself is often unconscious. If a man is offered a fact which goes against his instincts, he will scrutinize it closely, and unless the evidence is overwhelming, he will refuse to believe it. If, on the other hand, he is offered something which affords a reason for acting in accordance to his instincts, he will accept it even on the slightest evidence. The origin of myths is explained in this way.

—Bertrand Russell

Each of us has a significant number of beliefs we hold dear and are willing to defend with all our might. Other beliefs we hold have more flexibility and can be changed relatively easily. Ultimately every persuasion situation revolves around changing another person's beliefs at some level.

A simple belief that the majority of Americans would hold as being true is that freedom in all of its legal forms is the right of every American. Most people would be willing to defend that position as a nation no matter what the cost, because it is a core principle upon which our society is built. But one event can instantly shift people's beliefs. On September 11, 2001, when planes crashed into the World Trade Center in New York City, our beliefs about many things shifted in an instant. One of the most noticeable changes people were willing to accept without questioning (at least for a while) was restrictions of certain freedoms. Why? Because it was in our best interest to be safe rather than express our freedoms; we needed more information before we would go back to the previous levels of freedom.

While the above example is extreme to some, it in fact clearly demonstrates the persuasion process in a way anyone living in the United States can understand. The whole country wrestled with whether torture of suspected terrorists was now okay, something most people were at least theoretically against before. We suddenly had to wrestle with the idea of how much force our military, law enforcement and security agencies could use against another human being in order to extract information that might save thousands of lives. We were willing to examine our beliefs and change them in ways we had never considered.

There is a second part to beliefs as well: We all need something to believe in and we all want to believe in something bigger than ourselves. Even those who see themselves as being gods, are, in their own way, buying into a bigger belief system and idea than themselves; they need the reassurance that only belief can bring. Interestingly, many of our deeply held beliefs have no factual foundation. No one can prove the existence of a supreme God, but many millions of people worldwide find great comfort in that belief. Many people have beliefs that people are reincarnated after death or that there is life outside of our galaxy. None of those things can be conclusively proven, yet the comfort of the belief gives the believers common ground, a built-in set of friends and acquaintances, and a community; it creates a level of safety and can in many ways dictate behavior. Religious beliefs dictate the behavior of many. By following many different sets of beliefs we give our life structure, safety, and meaning.

Anyone who challenges our beliefs immediately comes under scrutiny and is often labeled a heretic. Many times scientists and researchers are ridiculed for daring to suggest that our long-held beliefs are no longer valid. We so desperately want to maintain our beliefs we will hamper progress to protect our precious beliefs.

I have spent a long time talking about beliefs and how they affect us for a very good reason. The biggest reason most persuasive arguments fail is that we fail to take a close look at the beliefs we are trying to change. Often we have the opinion we are simply trying to get people to take a slightly different action, but we fail to understand all of the deeply held beliefs that changing that action may affect.

Let us look at something as simple as a woman attempting to persuade her husband to put the toilet seat down. There is a logical argument to be made that it is a nice thing to do, that it looks better, that it makes her feel better, and a dozen other reasons for putting the seat down. On the other side of the equation, there is the argument that if it is that big of a deal the woman can put it down and that she should look before she sits down because the man looks and lifts the seat as necessary in order to use the facilities. And the argument can go on forever and does in many homes even today.

The issue is that the argument may go much deeper than simply why the seat should be up or down. Often when talking to one party or the other you find there are beliefs that make each position one that is unlikely to change. When you talk to the woman you find out she believes putting the seat down is a sign of a man being well-mannered and a gentleman. She also believes it is a sign her husband respects her because her father always did it for her mother. The husband on the other hand is a man's man. Since his father never put the seat down and defended his position to his mother, leaving the seat up is a sign that he is in control of the household and putting it down subverts his authority.

In order for either of the parties to get the other closer to agreement they have to understand what the beliefs are that they are working to change. Once you understand the belief and how closely held it is you can begin to develop an effective strategy to create change in the belief or to build a foundation that includes the belief. All too often we feel like we have to change the belief when incorporating it will do just fine. Taking advantage of the power of a belief and creating a better outcome based on using the belief is often much more effective.

When I sold point-of-sale software (the software that runs cash registers) there was a belief that the point-of-sale functionality must just do one thing—handle inventory and the sale transaction. Once that part was done, the information would then be entered into the accounting system and the accountants would work their magic from there. There were many things that related to extra work and possibility of data errors that made this a false belief, but it was the way things had been done since the turn of the century. Money went in the cigar box and change came out. At the end of the day you do the ledger.

There was only one problem with the belief for us. Our software was built around the idea that accounting and point of sale should be tied together. We needed to shift their belief. We could have spent millions of dollars creating advertising campaigns over years that would hopefully get people to think about the problem or we could just build on the belief that people already had, which is exactly what we did. Rather than position our product as an accounting package that also did point of sale, we built on the belief. We positioned the software as a point-of-sale software that optionally integrated with the accounting function if you wanted. You did not have to use the accounting function, but it was there. We made some very simple arguments about how much time it would save and how it would reduce data entry errors and left it at that. The result was that we built on the belief that the people who were using the software were already right and positioned our software to be congruent with their current beliefs. We also gave them some brief evidence that there were other possibilities that could be true if they wanted to investigate them.

The results were very interesting. We grew a product category by over 500 percent in one year. We also saw a proportionate increase in the number of users and tech-support buyers of our accounting product. Why? Simply because when people got the new software most attempted to defend their old belief by proving why it was right. The only way to prove it was right was to prove the new idea was wrong, which required them to try the software. As a result of trying the software, they experienced the results we wanted them to and their beliefs shifted nearly immediately. Today there is very little point-of-sale software that is not integrated with accounting. Massive change and new belief acceptance are what happen when you change beliefs.

We all have a desire to believe. When presented with new information, we typically believe what we see and hear immediately. This is called automatic believing. Until we run the belief through a series of tests to see if the new belief is actually true, we continue to believe the new information, a condition called belief perseverance.

We all have selective perception patterns that allow us to see things more as our beliefs say they are rather than as they really are. We set up mental structures or schemas that allow us to organize and simplify the information around us. Those models are overlaid onto ourselves, other people, what we like and dislike, and nearly everything we do.

Schemas act as filters that allow us to see or be blind to the various elements of a situation; they support our beliefs of what something we see should be. We have all had the experience of seeing someone dressed poorly and apparently not well-educated and judging him only to find when we spoke to him that he was actually very well-spoken and interesting, but was simply working in his yard or on his car. The problem for many of us is that we see one thing and instantly interpret it as being something that fits our schema rather than testing our belief to see if it holds true in this situation. In order to persuade effectively you have to suspend your models and beliefs long enough to test them to see if they hold true for the situation in which you are currently involved.

Another challenge of our beliefs and mental models of the world is that they will persist even when contradictory evidence exists because we tend to ignore that which does not match our interpretation.

If you hope to persuade effectively you must first examine the beliefs people hold true that are congruent to your position and get them to reaffirm their beliefs. Once beliefs are reaffirmed you have begun moving the people you are persuading into a place where you can reframe their belief to include your position.

You must also remain flexible in your own beliefs and regularly challenge your schemas as they relate to certain kinds of people or beliefs if you hope to change them. You must encourage people to challenge their own beliefs and introduce new ideas and supporting evidence you want them to consider.

The interesting thing about beliefs is that they can change slowly or very rapidly depending on the situation and condition of the person whose belief you are trying to change. When people have become sufficiently frustrated or stressed about a particular problem or event, they are very keen to grab onto a solution, any solution, and they find great emotional release in finding that solution. And that emotional release, that fulfillment, allows them to create a belief in an instant. This is one of the prime conversion techniques of cult recruiters and it will work as well for you when you begin to carefully study the areas of extreme frustration the person you hope to influence is experiencing. The desire for a release or salvation from some issue allows people to more readily (and quickly) change their beliefs.

All too often when we set out to persuade, we want to change the belief that another has to be the same as our belief. Rarely is it necessary to get people to fully believe your position or completely change theirs to get them to take the action you want.

Sometimes simply getting people to suspend their belief gives you the opportunity you need to introduce a new idea, and sometimes you simply want to create a question about the current belief. Ultimately your goal as a persuader is to create new beliefs and get people to change their existing beliefs in a way that allows them to accept your belief, too.

The hardest beliefs to change are those that rely heavily on faith or lack of evidence. Religious beliefs are the hardest to change for that exact reason. If you want to convert a Catholic to Mormonism, you have your work cut out even though on the surface they both believe the same thing fundamentally. You do not have to shift a big belief but you do need to move many smaller beliefs dramatically in order to get them to consider the idea. The other challenge with these kinds of beliefs it that they tend to be evaluated in absolute terms. (Mormonism is a cult, Catholicism is not, or vice versa depending on your beliefs.)

The issue of belief is one that advertisers wrestle with every day. How do I get you to leave the brand and all it means to you after 20 years of experience for another brand with which you have little experience? The answer, it turns out, is not as difficult as you might believe, but rarely is it applied appropriately.

Beliefs have a lot to do with memory, repetition, and credibility of the person delivering the new message. If I tell you there is a three-step process to changing beliefs there is a high likelihood you will accept that as fact because I'm an expert on persuasion. If you hear that same idea presented in numerous different media outlets it starts to become true and a belief you hold. When you start telling others about the process, you endorse the idea and the belief. The result is that the idea that there are three steps to changing beliefs becomes a widely accepted belief or common knowledge. There are many of those kinds of common beliefs we all share that, as it turns out, are absolutely not true. For example, have you ever heard that you lose 90 percent of your body heat through your head? If that were true, there would be no need for anything other than the lightest of clothes in the coldest part of winter as long as you wore a hat! But, now that I have challenged the belief, you have to think about it. If I suggest you do a test, for example, putting on a skimpy swimsuit and standing in the subzero conditions for an hour with only a stocking cap on, you immediately see the problem with the belief and will likely change it.

In essence I have just given you the belief creation and belief change process, but let me break it down a little more linearly so you can see how to create and change beliefs effectively.

SEVEN-STEP BELIEF CREATION AND CHANGE PROCESS

In order to create a new belief you have to present material in a credible way. The best way to present material is from the point of view of an expert. We are preconditioned in our society to not argue with experts, to listen to what they have to say and to accept their opinions because they have specialized knowledge that we do not. I explain more about how to become an expert in Chapter 6 on gurudom, but for now it is only important to understand that you need to present your material with confidence, conviction, and credibility whether or not you are an expert. The fact is, it is a little hard to argue that you are not the world's foremost expert on your opinion.

1. Elicit or identify the current belief that someone holds around the idea you are presenting. If you are an advertiser, you might demonstrate your knowledge of the belief that is held based on your current research. If you are selling one-on-one you may simply ask the question, "What is important to you about X?" People tend to express their beliefs about something when you ask that question, but if you are not sure why that is important, ask the clarifying question, "Why is that important to you?"
2. Identify areas of frustration or confusion around the issue.
3. Present the new idea or desired outcome you would like for your audience to have confidently and knowledgeably and back it up with credible evidence of truth. If you are trying to change a strongly held belief, you may need to demonstrate

your evidence a number of times and through a number of credible sources. In changing beliefs, once you make people aware of the new idea, it is important there is enough independent evidence that they will see it on their own. Because they have now become very conscious of the new idea they will be immediately attracted to the evidence that it is correct when they see it. They become immediately aware of all of the incidences of the truth around them. Be very careful here, though. If your position or product or service is controversial or negative in some way, they will also become aware of those incidences as well and it is much easier for them to maintain their existing beliefs than to take the time to sort out the real truth.

4. If your audience is still having difficulty changing, ask them if they would act "as if" they believed a certain thing for just a moment. Ask them what they would do differently and how they could do it. Acting "as if" forces them to at least temporarily accept the belief as their own, and once they have done that, they are well on the way to persuading themselves.

5. Reinforce the idea often and present them with situations where the idea is accurate and true.

6. Give them proof, let them sample your product or service, or show them testimonials of others who have had their same experience and changed their belief.

7. When they create the new belief or shift their belief, reward them for their behavior. Put them on the *inside* where they are part of an elite group, the President's club, or the preferred group. Follow up with them often to maintain the belief.

Once you have changed or created a new belief, it is much easier to persuade that person in the future because you've benefited him and he trusts you and you've now created another belief . . . that you now have a relationship and a shared commonality, and you both believe the same thing.

Remember, we all have a desire to believe in ideas and concepts bigger than ourselves or that better us in some way. We are most open to accepting those ideas and creating new beliefs when we have a particular need or question in mind. By understanding how important beliefs are and how many decisions are tied to beliefs that are deeply emotional rather than logical, we can increase our success in creating a persuasive environment.

 Chapter Review

☞ Beliefs are tied very closely to the positions that we hold and we will defend beliefs with all our might. Understanding what the beliefs are of the people you are trying to persuade allows you to focus on building on their current beliefs rather than trying to change them or create a new belief.

☞ People are most likely to change their beliefs when they are searching for a solution to a problem that has caused them stress, concern, or confusion. Emotional release allows them to create new beliefs quickly.

☞ You must present new ideas with conviction and credibility to create an environment where the new ideas can be accepted.

(Continued)

☛ Everyone wants to believe in something and it is the job of the persuader to position the idea that the people being persuaded can believe in and make their own.

☛ Those most willing to put their own beliefs or schemas aside will be in the best position to persuade others.

☚ Success Questions

☛ What beliefs do I currently hold that may hold me back?

☛ What is one specific incident where a difference in belief kept me from being able to persuade someone?

☛ What beliefs do I already share with the people I have to persuade?

☛ What idea or concept can I present that those I am persuading can believe in?

☛ Whom do I know or work with now whose beliefs I need to address in order to move our relationship forward?

☛ What evidence can I present that will reinforce the new belief I am presenting?

8

FAMILIARITY

Familiarity is the root of the closest friendships, as well as the intensest hatreds.

—Antoine Rivarol

The simple truth about familiarity as it relates to persuasion is this: The more familiar we are with people, places, events, products, services, or situations, the more likely we are to view them through a schema that is immediately either good or bad, depending on our previous experience.

In order to persuade effectively, you must identify what is familiar to the person or group that you hope to move. What common ground exists? What shared experiences are readily available as middle ground? To what groups or organizations do they belong? Whom do they hate or revile universally? Whom do they love? What experience do they all hope to have? By understanding what is familiar you can join them in the middle ground of shared experience or desire.

When we open dialog from an area of common ground, even

95

a common physical location, we force people to begin observing the situation from a familiar schema. We put them in a place emotionally where they will experience old feelings and ideas. In selling, this is the concept of pain and pleasure: the idea that people will move away from pain and toward pleasure. We can build on either positive or negative schemas depending on the direction we need to move.

A number of years ago I was working with a very large client who was in the midst of rolling out a new point-of-sale system. Their business was very seasonal and over 60 percent of their annual volume was done in a 45-day selling period. One of the challenges we had was getting the product set up appropriately in mall kiosks because they typically were not set up by trained technical staff, which resulted in a high number of support calls to the client's internal support people. Regardless of where the fault lies, when internal support gets a high number of calls, the client tends to shift that blame back to the vendor, which is exactly what happened.

I knew in order to keep the project on track and to keep the issue from spiraling out of control, I had to persuade the director of information technology and support to accept responsibility and find a more effective way of getting the units installed. My initial attempts met with resistance. After talking for a while, I discovered that both of us had a shared experience as enlisted men in the military. The minute I found that out I began to frame this experience around our shared experiences at having surmounted impossible tasks with equipment that was substandard and people who did not know how to use it. I got him involved in telling me about his biggest military nightmare and how he had solved it. After I got him fully emotionally charged about that event, I moved him back to the issue at hand, getting these units installed properly. Nearly immediately I shifted his thought process from "One of us wins and one of us loses" to "We are in this together; how can we make it work?" Within 10 minutes he had developed a solution (with a little gentle guidance) that would make the process work. At the end of our conversation, he said, "You know, these guys need to get creative just like we used to; they need to understand that they are getting paid to solve problems. I'm going to get to work on that right away." The result was a very successful season and a relationship with the client's point-of-sale provider that lasts to this day.

Finding familiar ground will help the persuasive process, as I have just demonstrated. It is much easier to persuade someone with whom you have bonded, with whom you have a relationship, than someone you have just met. But beware; it is also very easy to be persuaded by that person, so be sure you are not giving ground when you should not.

Get to know the people you hope to persuade. The more personal you can become with them, the better. Learn what their likes and dislikes are; understand their schemas as they relate to sales, persuasion, your product, your industry, and anything that might give you a little bit of an edge later. Be certain that you understand their pain and the problems they are hoping to solve.

It is also good to let them get to know you a little. You should always know the person you are persuading better than they know you. They should know your public persona and reputation and a little about you personally so they feel like they are on the inside track, but never enough that they have an edge with you. You need to maintain a little distance while creating a sense of familiarity in order to be successful. In a 1999 *New York Times*/CBS News poll, those surveyed said that they expected 85 percent of the people they knew personally to act fairly.

That one survey demonstrates how important it is to get to know people and let them become familiar with you. Interestingly, the more you know about someone, regardless of how much they know about you, the more familiar they feel with you. Take the time to get to know the people you hope to persuade. If you cannot get to know them personally then, at a minimum, get to know them as best you can informally through research before you meet them so you can ask well-planned questions that will draw them in quickly.

As humans, we like to hear about ourselves and we like to know that others know about us. By doing your research on Google ahead of time you can find a great many references to people that they may not even know exist. Google now has a new tool called Google Answers that will allow you to bid from $1 to $200 for research to be done for you. In researching this book I found a lot of valuable resource material for less than $5 and typically got very detailed answers. Of course, if you don't want to do all the work yourself, research librarians will still do much of your work for you at no charge as well. Ultimately, since there is no better source of information than those people closest to the person you hope to know, use your network to identify people you know in common and gather as much information as you can in advance.

Once you have gathered your information, use it. Direct the conversation in the way that brings around critical pieces of information you have gathered. Use them to demonstrate your knowledge of the person or their positions but only for the point of asking more detailed questions that allow you to create rapport and gather more information personally. Share a little of your own information as necessary to facilitate the conversation; share the common ground, the common friends, or the common experience to create a sense of being someone familiar. Post-conversation follow-up is a great way of anchoring that sense of familiarity to you. Be sure to drop a note or make a phone call.

FAMILIARITY IN ACTION

One of the things I always do at tradeshows, for example, is write down at least one thing I learned about people on the back of their business cards. Then, when I'm at the airport waiting to head to my next location, I organize the cards from most important to least. The most important people get a phone call from the airport and I say something like this: "Dan, this is Dave Lakhani from Bold Approach; I'm just sitting here at the airport thinking about our conversation about the Shriners. It seems like there are fewer and fewer of us around so it is always great to meet someone new. Thanks for spending a few moments with me at your booth. I hope the show went exceptionally well for you and I look forward to speaking with you next week to follow up on our conversation. You know, I'm curious about one thing, have you ever visited the Shriner's Children's Hospital in Salt Lake City? I'll be curious to find out more about your experiences with the Shrine as well. Have a great day; if you'd like to reach me prior to next week, here is my number; I'll be excited to take your call."

That simple phone call reinforcing our common ground has led to many great relationships for me that were profitable both professionally and personally. I can find something in common with nearly anyone. It might be a sports team we follow, a militar connection, a fraternal connection, growing up or living in certain regions of the country or the world, or simply that we both have daughters.

You can find commonality and familiarity in just about anything. When I see where someone's company is located I ask if they are from that city originally. Sometimes the answer is yes, but often it is no and with the no comes an explanation about how they got from wherever they came from to where they are today. That simple question gives you a great deal of information that you can incorporate to find common ground you can use to create familiarity. Familiarity is another way of borrowing credibility and power from a person, situation, organization, or event to strengthen your position.

When persuading groups when you do not have time to develop high levels of familiarity, take advantage of the shared experiences you have all had. Virtually everyone sitting in front of you has had the experience of being in boring meetings or listening to speakers who drone on. Talk about that experience and what you will do to make it different. Give them tangible signs. They will be able to relate to what makes meetings tough, like the uncomfortable chair or the person with the big hair blocking their view. Then, move them forward to other familiar ground by letting them know how you are going to make the experience different this time. Create a new shared experience that you lead.

No matter whom you persuade or how you do it, take the time now to examine your relationships and see which would benefit from establishing a higher level of familiarity and get to work. Every effort you invest in creating a more familiar environment and creating a level of comfort and familiarity will pay you back tenfold.

Chapter Review

☞ We tend to like and trust people who are like us.

☞ Familiarity breeds trust.

☞ Always get to know something about every person you hope to persuade. In this case, it is better to receive (information) than to give. The person with the most information about the other holds the biggest set of cards in the game of persuasion.

☞ Try to move all of your persuasive conversations from a shared commonality to a new shared experience that you will create together.

 ## Success Questions

☞ In which relationships should I increase familiarity?

☞ What questions can I ask that will help me more quickly find common ground and create a sense of familiarity?

☞ What are the most common shared experiences I have had that I can use to quickly create familiarity?

☞ What are the common problems everyone faces who needs my products or services?

☞ Whom do I have in common with someone I want to deeply influence today that I can look to for an insider's view of the person I am persuading?

EXCLUSIVITY AND AVAILABILITY

It is not worth an intelligent man's time to be in the majority.
By definition, there are already enough people to do that. . . .

—G.H. Hardy

EXCLUSIVITY

Everyone has a desire to be exclusive. We not only want to be unique and individuals, but we want to be unique in the groups we belong to, the cars we drive, and the clothes we wear. Going to a prestigious school or belonging to an elite membership club has been a key that opens many doors for those who belong. In government and national security, Yale's Skull and Crossbones club stands out. Many successful businessmen and politicians are Freemasons.

It is not simply the idea that you are different (though that is certainly a part) alone that makes people crave exclusivity. It is the desire to be able to have access to others like you. When you belong to exclusive organizations, everywhere you go you have a friend or at least someone with something in common. Even if you cannot find someone who belongs to the group, you can find people who are desirous of belonging.

Because the desire for exclusivity is so compelling, every person should have an "inner circle." An inner circle is a group of people who have special access to you, to knowledge, or even to products and services that no one else has. Many businesses and nonprofit organizations alike have professional or volunteer boards that help them govern their organizations. Serving on boards is a very powerful and exclusive move for a persuader to make. When your peers and those you hope to influence see that you are sitting on a board your stature is elevated in their eyes in many cases. Being on a board also gives you another level of exclusive access, not just to the company executives and other board members, but members of other boards. Serving in an exclusive capacity is another way of enhancing your persona while at the same time giving you additional access.

Boards provide another function. They give you the opportunity to create an exclusive group of advisors to whom you would like to have ready access. Mastermind groups, as popularized by Napoleon Hill in his famous book, *Think and Grow Rich* (Fawcett, NY, 1969), are very exclusive groups, many of which are nearly impossible to get into.

Nonprofits take advantage of this exclusivity regularly to raise more money. People who donate may get their name in the paper, but people who donate larger sums get special recognition—maybe they are silver members and are denoted as such in the paper. The highest-level donors may be marked out in a separate section of the thank-you and given plaques and awards for their generosity. The only way to join them, of course, is to donate at the same level.

Today I have an inner circle consisting of some of the very best advisors in the world. You would most certainly recognize their names and would love to have access to these people. The only way you would ever get to meet them is the same way I did, by having someone endorse me as an important addition to the group and then give me a chance to prove my value.

I also have an inner circle of clients who have exclusive access to some of my most carefully guarded material and with whom I regularly communicate personally and typically one-on-one to ensure their persuasive success. I reject more than half the people who want to be a part of this group because they are not a good fit ethically, emotionally, financially, or from a similarity standpoint. I want only the most dedicated, profitable, and highly motivated people in that group. Why? The answer is simple. That is where progress really happens—where deals are made and where specific-need persuasion strategy is developed and tested.

Some of the top salespeople and negotiators in the world belong to this group and they demand their exclusivity not be diluted. As a result, there are never more than 100 people who are members of this particular group worldwide. Someone literally has to quit or die before you could even be considered. But those 100 people are responsible for millions of dollars in commerce each year. Imagine what would happen for you if you had that level of access to some of the greatest minds and most unbelievable Rolodexes in the United States today. Trust me when I say the opportunities are nearly beyond imagination.

Did you notice how much your desire to belong increased as I explained the group to you? Do you see how the curiosity I created caused you to wonder if you could qualify? Did you begin to imagine a little of what might happen for your business if you were able to join? Some people will answer no and that is okay, because those people would not be a good fit. When we create something exclusive we want very specific people involved. Typically the people we do not want will not find the exclusivity appealing in the first place.

In persuasion, exclusivity is important for another reason. Exclusivity is predictable. Those people who belong are much more likely to follow the action of the group than people who are on the outside. Members are much more likely to respond positively to special offers and to requests for assistance, introductions, or referrals.

The question you have to ask yourself is "How do I create exclusivity for those I wish to persuade?" The answer for most is relatively simple. You can start out by creating an event with limited opportunity for attendance. It might be the unveiling of a new product or it could be the announcement of a major change in your company. You can create a board of directors and invite those people whom you want to influence most deeply to be a part or you can create a mastermind group with very exclusive membership.

There are many ways of creating exclusivity for your clients and here are a few ideas that you can start with:

- ☞ Create a special group that are the recipients of very specific information or special offers limited to them, or given to them in advance of everyone else.
- ☞ Create a controlled membership group that gives them access to other people or opportunities that would otherwise not be available.
- ☞ Create a club or group they can belong to wherever they are that is exclusive to their tastes. The Red Hat Society

and *Fast Company* magazine's Company of Friends are great examples. Women who are over 50 (and younger) who want to celebrate life before they are old get together regularly (wearing their red hats) to sip tea and talk. *Fast Company's* Company of Friends lets its like-minded readers meet on a regular basis to network with one another. Both are restricted to people who want to exclusively identify themselves in public with the hope of some gain. The gain they receive may only be emotional, but may also be financial.

☞ Create a program in which people must specifically qualify to belong or to take part.

☞ Simply limit particular sales or offers to those people who have spent large sums with you over the past year. Let them know that you have created a special program for a group of people like them and tell them what they get as a result.

☞ Create a list of people who get through to you no matter what . . . then let them know they are on it.

Exclusivity is tied closely to identity. Your clients or people that you hope to persuade want to be distinguished in a certain way. They go well out of their way to be sure people know who they are and for what they stand. By simply observing their behavior and determining what they desire to be known for, you are better able to position your exclusive opportunity so it matches their desires perfectly.

Remember that there is a difference between exclusive and secret. There are very few people who do not want to be known for what they do. The majority of people, no matter how small their group or how altruistic their goals, want some recognition for belonging. They may like a little mystery around what they do and how they do it, but they want people to desire to belong (if they did not, it would be a very short-lived organization). Nearly all want entry to be controlled and want to feel that it takes a certain amount of effort to become a part of it all.

AVAILABILITY

Short supply motivates people to action. Nearly every year at Christmas there is one toy that everyone has to have . . . and by the time they find out it is sold out. No matter, though, people will go to great extremes to get the desirable yet unavailable toy. They will pay 10 and sometimes 100 times the price just to get it. Another example of scarcity that we have all experienced is the auction. Items many times sell for as much as or more than they cost new because someone is afraid they will miss out on getting the product (and the great deal) that they want.

For the masterful persuader availability can be a very valuable tool in encouraging your prospects to take action right away. You should use availability in two ways. The first is to limit actual product availability. The second is to limit the number of products available at a specific price or the number available with specific incentives for taking advantage of your offer immediately.

A very interesting thing happens when you begin to control availability; you also create exclusivity. The person who is able to actually get your product or get your product with all the add-on incentives has something only a few others have.

Another way of increasing desirability through controlling availability is through a sliding pricing strategy. If you purchase today the price is $99, if you wait and purchase tomorrow it goes up to $125, and if you wait until Friday, the price is $150. With each day that passes there is more and more pressure to buy for those people who sit on the fence.

Virtually every time I use this strategy people will contact me after the last day with some excuse about why they were not able to get in but should get the original price. They want the product but they waited too long. Usually, I won't give it to them at the lower price because I want them to make a more rapid decision the next time I make the offer. If they have a legitimate reason that they could not take advantage of the offer and I have products left, then I may consider giving them the lower price. The problem with limiting availability and then giving a lower price to someone who did not take advantage in a timely manner is that you condition them to not take advantage. They know they can come back and get it later at the same price. Many Internet marketers make the mistake of having a sale, then extending a sale and then offering the lower price to anyone who asks for it. That is simply a recipe for never getting your desired profit margin and for creating bad customers.

Discounting is technically limiting the availability of a price. You must be careful when discounting to not condition people to think it will always be there or the technique backfires. One of the nation's largest craft stores does this every Sunday. You can look in the Sunday paper in any town that this chain is in and there is always a coupon for 40 percent off one item. There is no reason to ever pay full price for anything in the store, especially not large purchases. I understand the argument about the people who will come in and get 40 percent off but spend a lot more and when they do it is great. I prefer to condition my buyers differently. I would give the discount to preferred customers who I know will stay with me based on their buying habits and reward them for their loyalty. Customers who regularly respond to percent-off deals do so with your competitors too.

Availability also applies to building your persona. Limiting access to yourself and even the information about how to reach you personally creates exclusivity and a stronger sense of urgency to reach you and do business when the opportunity presents itself.

It is vitally important that you do not use this technique as a means of avoiding the people you should be talking to. It is simply a way of reinforcing the idea that you are busy and in demand. Professionals worth their fees are not easy to get to; they are too busy helping their loyal clients.

One strategy is to control your appointment calendar. Be sure that you tell your receptionist who you will always take calls from and which times during the day you have available to talk. It is important to carefully script what you want your receptionist to say as well. You want the message to be, "The only time available on John's calendar today is at three forty-five P.M.; I can fit you in for fifteen minutes then for an initial call. Will that work for you?" There is great urgency to get that spot on the calendar. Always have your receptionist give the caller one option for today if you are available and one for the following day or the next day you are available.

Right now I know some of you are saying, "I don't have a receptionist. I answer my own calls." Stop right now and get one. You can hire an answering service or receptionist service online for pennies a day. A lot of executives will tell you they answer their own phones and they do. The only people who have their direct lines are the people who they have already made feel exclusive by giving them a direct line. If you absolutely insist on answering your own phone follow the same process. Set a time later in the day or the following one to get on your calendar.

Whether you are creating a fanatical cult or a cult of customers, exclusivity and availability are keys to your success. Customers want a payoff; they want to be on the inside track and they want to be rewarded for their uniqueness and quick action. When I was growing up in a cult the reward was access to heaven and everlasting life. Equally powerful was the opportunity to speak with or spend time with our minister. Once you spent time with him you were special, you were on the inside and exclusive. From that point on, believing him was easy. It was also the ability to be separate from a world that was believed to be on its way to hell. Availability was very limited too; if I did not choose now there was every likelihood that tomorrow would be too late.

What is it you can give your customers that they can form around and believe in? Find that, and let in those customers who want it. Don't worry; the group will grow because those who belong will be the missionaries who recruit others to be just like them. And, you already know how much easier it is to persuade once the transfer of power and credibility has occurred.

 Chapter Review

☞ The more exclusive you can make someone feel, the more likely they are to be persuaded.

☞ Exclusive groups are easier to persuade than generic groups.

☞ Exclusivity is one of the keys to building a cult, whether a cult of customers or of brands.

☞ Exclusivity is closely tied to identity. Reinforce the tie between people's identities and the exclusivity and you move them much more quickly and easily to your point of view.

Success Questions

☞ Who in my sphere of influence, customer base, or prospect base should I make exclusive?

☞ What can I create that will get people to identify themselves as belonging, for example, a newsletter list or a special edition club?

☞ What exclusive groups do I already belong to that I can share access to with people I want to persuade?

 10

CURIOSITY

The first and simplest emotion which we discover in the human mind, is curiosity.

—Edmund Burke

Curiosity killed the cat, but satisfaction brought it back.

—Eugene O'Neill

In terms of persuasive emotions, curiosity is king. Most sales and persuasion books will tell you pain and pleasure are key emotions but that is only partially right. You cannot move in either direction until you are first curious if there is a lower low or a higher high. Curiosity is the first emotion that we learn; it is the basis on which all of our current knowledge and experience is built. Curiosity is the impetus to change.

Many times the reason people are not persuaded is that they are not first made properly curious. Understand, there is no reason for people to change a current opinion of anything until they become curious about what other options might exist. Questions are one of the best tools for creating high levels of curiosity. Questions also allow you to lead people to the conclusions you desire.

If you want to deeply persuade people you must first find out what they are curious about. What would make them even consider that their opinion could be wrong or not efficient? More importantly, how will they know when they have made a good decision? By just knowing those two things, you will put yourself ahead of all your competition.

One of the first questions I ask when I am persuading is some version of the question "How will you define success or how will you know?" Everyone has an outcome that he must have in any decision he will make. The majority of people who will not make decisions do not because they have no idea how they will know when they have achieved success. The really interesting thing about this question is that it makes people intensely curious because they have rarely considered the answer. That gap where they have to think requires that they become curious. They have to ask themselves questions and find answers. For you, this is the perfect time to bring up new ideas because they are already in a curious state of mind. I cannot stress enough how important it is for you to get anyone you ever persuade to define how he or she will know "when."

"How do you know" gets to the core of the criteria that people have for the product, service, or even idea that they have. When you can get people to describe exactly what they want, you are halfway to "how will you know when." The second part of the process is getting them to tell you how they will know their decision was the right one. It is important that you understand how they will know they made the right decision so you can be sure the solution you are leading them to is one they will stay persuaded about.

There are many ways to create and enhance curiosity. Making

provocative statements that require questions begins moving the person you are persuading to be curious. Provocative statements can include very surprising facts or assumptions about the product, service, or concept you are discussing. Often by making a startling statement you force people into thinking about your topic in a new way. If you help someone create a new way of thinking, curiosity and questions are inevitable. Statements that require questions, again, put people in the position of needing to have more information, and if you have positioned yourself well, you will be their primary source of information.

Detailed information can also cause intense curiosity. When we are confronted with new information we do not understand, we must investigate and decide. During that time when our minds are open, we are most susceptible to change. In those moments, it is time to create a new level of curiosity about old beliefs and new solutions.

Direct questioning of assumptions and beliefs is a very effective technique for creating a high level of curiosity. In order to question assumptions appropriately you must use a reasonable amount of tact. There is a significant difference between questioning an assumption and challenging it. Challenges tend to be more confrontational in nature and put people on the defensive. Direct questioning, on the other hand, encourages people to open up and explain their ideas or beliefs. When they open up, it gives you the opportunity to ask more penetrating questions designed to get them to reconsider and perhaps question their position. Many people, when directly questioned, will admit to not knowing exactly why they believe something or will admit to holding a conviction that is that of their parents or spouse. Only through direct questioning can you appear to be genuine in your desire to learn while gathering valuable information you can use to persuade. You also have the opportunity, by the direction of your questions, to bring them to your point of view or predetermined conclusion.

Leaving important pieces of information out of your story, but alluding to them, is another way of creating curiosity. Leaving information out, but alluding to it, or giving information and then suggesting outright that we will give them additional information is a variation on the direct questioning technique. When we give only partial information, we let people fill in the blanks. It is important to test if you allow them to fill in the blanks to be sure that they filled the blank correctly. If they have not or if they do not get curious and ask you more questions, you must go back and give them the information so that they do not leave without the full story. The idea of omission is only to make them think and query. In Chapter 5 on storytelling I use this exact technique to make you intensely curious.

Let me give you a special password that gets people curious right away. Simply ask them what they are curious about. Be sure you use the word *curious* because it immediately requires them to become curious when they have to ponder what they are curious about. I often ask the question, What is the one thing you are really curious about in relation to this product or service? If we were face-to-face right now, I would ask you the question, What is it about persuasion that you are most curious about? Then I would wait for your answer. Once you gave me the answer I would ask you if there was anything else. That simple follow-on question again moves you back into an internal questioning process and will many times uncover more information.

One of the keys to building an effective cult is to have all of the answers. It is very easy to appear to have all of the answers when you direct the questions and the curiosity. When you have established yourself as an expert, you have great opportunity to direct the questions. Ideally you will ask the kind of questions that can only be answered affirmatively by your product or service. In a cult, many of those questions require intense thought and study. Of course, if you control the questions, it is also very easy to control the answers and the resources by which someone could find the answer. Ultimately in a cult, anything that cannot be explained requires faith.

In business or personal relationships anything that cannot be explained requires further study. The more study that is required, the more opportunity you have to direct the discovery. Why? The answer is very simple. People are very limited on time and want to be led. They like to be curious for a moment but they want instant satisfaction. That desire for satisfaction allows them to hang on to the first solution that makes sense to them.

One of the best ways to see how curiosity works is in the relationship between a man and a woman. If you want to date another person simply make him or her curious. People have an innate desire to learn about someone they see as an enigma. It is nearly impossible for them not to try and unpeel the layers just to see if their curiosity can be satisfied. If you do nothing during their discovery process they will discover just what they need to make a decision. But, if you make them curious, give them clues and some satisfaction while replacing it with more mystery, you create more desire to know. The more time people spend with you (and pondering you) the more familiar you become. Rather than seeing you as a person who is pursuing them, they become the seeker of knowledge. And when they are curious, they are susceptible to persuasion.

Cultists and serial manipulators know this and prey on it. They make discovery of the truth easy, but only through a process that brings you deeper and deeper into their grips. They allow you to question in the beginning and give you the answers you need, but eventually, as you become more comfortable, you stop questioning and start relating. At that point they have accomplished exactly what they desired. In order to back out, you have to start reevaluating your decisions and unless you are intensely curious you do not restart the questioning process.

One important thing to remember is that curiosity for the sake of curiosity can delay decisions. Be sure when you initiate curiosity that you have a plan that will lead the person you are persuading to the information you want her to discover and to the decisions you want her to make. The purpose of curiosity for the persuader is to crack the tough shell of belief and reverse unthinking tradition.

 Chapter Review

☛ Create curiosity wherever you can; curiosity is the oil that greases the wheels of change.

☛ To create curiosity ask good questions; directly question assumptions and beliefs.

☛ Remember that when people are curious change is possible.

☛ The purpose of curiosity is for you to direct the discovery of new information that will help others make the only logical decision they can . . . and the one you want them to make.

(Continued)

Success Questions

☞ What questions can I ask that will make my prospects intensely curious?

☞ What do the majority of prospects not know or understand that if they did would make them draw a new conclusion?

☞ What information can I leave out that will cause my prospects to ask good questions?

☞ What information can I allude to that will cause them to draw the correct conclusion required to fill in the blanks?

 11

RELEVANCY

*Your pitch or idea had better be immediately relevant to me or
I'll destroy you with apathy.*

—Dave Lakhani

A common reason that people are not persuaded by
what you have to say is that it is not relevant and does
not apply to them. One quick look at your mailbox
will reveal any number of offers that are directed to
you because you appear to meet certain criteria. The real problem is that they are in no way relevant to you. The problem is
made worse by the amount of unwanted e-mail or "spam" we receive on a daily basis.

Relevancy is all about providing me with information I need
now based on my own revealed needs and desires. Relevancy
goes much deeper when speaking of persuasion. It also applies to
the kinds of messages we send. You have to ask yourself how I
see myself in order to know what is relevant to me. You also need
to adjust your persona, whether in person or via any advertising
outlet, to appeal to me specifically.

Relevancy also means that you have taken the time to get to know me, to understand me as an individual or as a specific group, so that you can serve me better. It means you understand what is important to me in my life, in my job, in my free time, in my most private moments. It also means you understand my timing and know when your offer or idea will be most applicable to me. It does not necessarily mean that you know me personally, but you have studied me by studying many others like me. You ask questions more often than you provide information and when you do provide information it is tailored to my needs specifically. You can nearly read my mind because you understand almost as well as I do what I need and what I will get out of the relationship with someone like you. Once you have done that, you have begun to become relevant to me. There is a very short path between your relevancy and our mutually beneficial relationship.

A recent study done by Yankelovich Partners as reported at the American Association of Advertising Agencies by J. Walker Smith (April 15, 2004, American Association of Advertising Agencies Conference, Miami, FL) showed that 59 percent of people surveyed felt that "most marketing and advertising has little relevancy to them." Additionally the survey revealed that 33 percent would be willing to have a slightly lower standard of living to live in a society without marketing and advertising.

It is insane if not bordering on criminal to think that you can persuade anyone of anything they have no interest in. Unfortunately we often attempt that on a daily basis. The old idea that "sales and persuasion is a numbers game" is still so predominant that a significant amount of marketing falls on deaf ears. The real problem is not that your attempts are falling on deaf ears, but that people hear you and each piece of irrelevant information is another straw on the camel's back that eventually causes it to break. The result is that people become not just defensive, but also apathetic. The best way to not be persuaded is to be apathetic about whatever another person is talking to you about. Apathy takes a long time to build but takes an even longer time to turn around.

If you hope to persuade one single person or a stadium full of people, you must be sure that the information you are sharing is relevant to their needs and desires. Pay careful attention to what I said, "relevant to *their* needs and desires."

Each person you speak to will have different needs and desires; it is up to you to identify what those are specifically so you can address them. You also need to be sure that you are targeting the right person with your persuasive message or argument. There is no value at all in trying to persuade anyone of anything in which she has no interest. There is no product, service, or argument that applies to everyone universally and even if it did, each person or group would have their own specific needs and desires that would need to be addressed to make it appropriate for them.

The very best question you can ask yourself is this: "What makes this person a good match for my message?" By answering that simple question you will improve your odds of finding exactly the right person or people for your message.

The most repulsive person I ever worked for managed a large technology consulting firm. On top of being wildly dishonest and unethical, he thought virtually every person he or we talked to should switch their business to his company or should open their Rolodex to us. Even when there was not a match in expertise, he would encourage his sales teams to present other services that were in no way related to the prospect's current needs during presentations that were highly relevant to their needs. He would stand in the room and at the end of a presentation start quizzing everyone in the room about who they knew who could help him find more prospects in certain lines of business. In addition to the timing being horrible, most of the people in the room could not care less about his needs. Those people had one specific agenda and it did not involve giving him more business. It would be a little like going to your doctor and having him ask you before he goes if you know anyone who is going to be buying a car soon because he also sells cars. All credibility is destroyed. It was a perfect example of how failing to be relevant can destroy opportunities to win business.

Now don't get me wrong. I am not suggesting that you should not ask for leads, but there is a time and a place for it. Asking for leads is part of the sales process. The timing of the request for leads comes when there has been a successful conclusion of business. The other time is when the person you are asking has decided to not do business with you for reasons other than some inability to perform on your part.

When you are looking at a group of people you want to persuade, ask these questions:

☞ Have these people demonstrated a desire or need for my product or service?
☞ Do these people have a need for my product but don't recognize it? Do they remain unaware a problem exists?
☞ Is my product relevant in terms of their desires—financially and experientially?

☞ If you are trying to be relevant to a group of people, have you gathered the right group of people? Will at least half of them have knowledge, experience, or problems similar to the specific ones that your product, service, or idea can address?

☞ Have you carefully qualified your list before you start calling on people for any reason? No longer are generalizations enough (40+-year-old males, income $70,000+ per year, own a sports car); you must be much more specific (35–45-year-old male, income of $100,000 minimum, drives a Porsche Boxster or BMW Z3, buys suits at least once a month). The more you know about the prospect, the more likely you will be relevant.

At the end of the day, if you can clearly identify me, you have a high likelihood of being able to craft a presentation or idea that is relevant to me. The final step is being sure *you* are relevant to me. If your persona and style do not match my criteria for relevancy in a person I would trust, listen to, buy from, or have a relationship with, you become irrelevant. Once you become irrelevant, you don't get a second chance with me.

When you set out to persuade be sure that you understand what expectations exist in your potential client. Ask them what they expect if you do not know. There is no better way to become relevant than by asking better questions of the person you hope to influence. Relevancy starts with concern. If I feel you are concerned about me and my needs, you are more relevant to me than someone who "just wants a few minutes of my time to see if I might have a need for their services."

Be relevant or be gone.

Chapter Review

☞ When unqualified, more than half of the people you attempt to persuade will feel that what you have to say is not relevant to them.

☞ Relevancy and familiarity are closely linked. If you are relevant to me it is because you know something about me and the more you know about me the more familiar you feel.

☞ Spend your time carefully selecting whom you will persuade or to whom you will send your message. It is a little like the old carpenter's adage, "measure twice, cut once."

☞ Be sure your persona, style, and presentation match me, my lifestyle, my business, or my personality and you will become instantly more relevant.

 Success Questions

☞ What am I currently doing to insure that my message is going to the right person or group?

☞ What are the most important issues guaranteed to be facing my audience?

☞ How can I become more knowledgeable of those I hope to persuade?

☞ What can I do to develop niche groups in the masses I am currently working with and become intensely relevant to them?

 12

PERMISSION GRANTING

As we let our light shine, we consciously give other people per-mission to do the same. As we are liberated from our own fear, our presence actually liberates others.

— Marianne Williamson

This topic is often the most misunderstood when I speak to groups. It seems a little egotistical for me to believe that I can give you permission to do business with me. But each of you are silently begging me to give you permission if I have done a good job of creating curios-ity, desire, exclusivity, and scarcity. Your emotions are screaming, "Let me in, I want to be a part of this," and logic is finding a way to justify your decision.

Permission granting is another way of saying close the sale or bring the persuasion to a logical conclusion in your favor. There is just one slight difference. When you "close" a sale, you are ask-ing someone to do business with you and they still have all the power. When you grant permission, you are giving them a limited time opportunity to begin a relationship with you; you retain the power. Permission once given can also be taken away. In cult terms you can excommunicate someone whom you have granted permission, but firing a customer is much more difficult. Excommunicated people often repent and work very hard to get back in your good graces so they can be a part of the group again; fired people rarely do.

As I studied cults I realized this was one of the reasons my mom wrestled with her decision to leave for so long after she left and was excommunicated. There was that nagging worry, of course, that they might have been right, but more important was the acceptance and the comfort the group brought. There was the idea that she bought so fully into and could never excommunicate herself from as long as anyone she was familiar with was still involved. The problem was that they could easily remind her of all of the feelings of curiosity and desire that brought her there in the first place; she was still searching for the answers that eluded her. Many of the people she knew and considered friends were still involved in seeking and living the best answer she had found. The result was that the pull to go back remained strong long after logic dictated she had made a fine decision to leave and was living a normal life. Interestingly, Mom never felt she could have the positive beliefs about God and religion that were shared with the cult (not everything they believed was bad, although the vast majority was) without their permission and acceptance.

THE IMPORTANCE OF PERMISSION GRANTING

Permission granting is an important distinction for you to understand because of the position of power it places you in. Permission granting also skews the relationship in your favor because only people with authority whom we have exalted to some level (gurudom) can give us permission. So once you have placed yourself in the position that you can grant permission, you have also placed yourself in a trusted advisor's position. The only way that will change is if you do something that is so incongruent or wrong that the prospect has to reevaluate you completely. Short of that, you are in position to have significant influence in the part of that person's life that relates to what you do.

You have often heard that people are silently begging to be led, that they are waiting for you to tell them what to do. That is very true when it comes to persuasion. The majority of people who are buying anything want you not only to tell them what to do but to reassure them they are making the right decision. Once that is done, the very last thing they need is for you to tell them it is okay. They need the reassurance of permission in order to metaphorically close their eyes and fall backwards safely into your arms without fear of injury. All you have to do is simply facilitate the process. They will have convinced themselves this is what they want—they just want you to tell them to do it. When you tell people to do anything with you, you are giving your permission for them to do it. If I invite you into my house you have my permission and if I invite you to be a part of my closest and most trusted customer base, you now have my permission. Permission feels very good and comforting.

There are many psychological reasons that permission granting is one of those ideas that we simply accept and follow without thought, but think of it this way. Remember when you were young and you had to have permission to get up from the table or to go to the restroom at school? You had to ask if it was okay and once you got permission, there were no more consequences, because you had permission from a higher authority. As a persuader, once you give permission, the person you are persuading is absolved from wrong because you, the higher authority, gave your permission.

There are many subliminal ways of granting permission. One of the best is the guarantee. If I guarantee that something will work or that some action will occur, you now have my permission to take action because if it does not work you have another form of absolution. Remember what happened when you got caught in the hallway at school by the hall monitor or principal? You were challenged but you could answer the challenge because you had permission to be there. If your permission was challenged you resolved it by going to the granting authority and proving your position. Guarantees work in much the same way. When your spouse or boss challenges your decision, you can answer the challenge of risk by showing that you have a guarantee. You have permission to make this decision because if it is the wrong one you can still have absolution. You have a guarantee.

Another covert permission tactic is the test drive or trial. Whenever I give you a test drive or a trial you have my permission to take the product and prove it will work for you just the way I said it would. You also have permission to buy it because I brought you into the group. You are now part of the group that has leather furniture in every room of their home or who has the special bed or who drives a Porsche Boxster. You have the permission of all the other people like you to join the club. You have the reassurance (and permission) of the group when you pull up next to someone else at a light who is driving a Porsche and they give you that knowing look and nod. You have permission to never change the moment someone asks you about your car because they have reinforced in a way no salesman can that you are special and envied . . . even if you are just on a test drive.

A more overt way of giving permission is to simply tell people what you want them to do next. You tell them the process they need to go through and then start them on the process. You simply assume (this is like the assumptive close in sales training) they are going to do something and that they have the authority to take the action you are now helping them take. By simply helping people do something as simple as start a process and respecting and acknowledging their authority, you have given them permission to take action.

I have even gone so far as to tell people, "Hey, you have my permission to do this," in a joking way. You have to be *very* sure that you do it in a nonthreatening and joking way and that you have deep rapport with the person before you do it. That simple permission, while it seems to be a little aggressive and almost funny to think about, really does work at a subconscious level. It is just like Mrs. Smith, who used to give you permission to go to the restroom in the first grade, giving you permission to spend a million dollars on the new IT project. This kind of approach is best used when someone is really on the fence, when they really want to make the decision but just cannot quite pull the trigger.

In negotiations and other nonproduct-oriented persuasion situations it is often very effective to give permission by asking people to "act as if." A very good technique to use is simply asking people if they would mind going through a quick creative thinking process with you. I say, "I learned this really effective technique for making good decisions and I'd like you to go through it with me right now." Then I continue, "I'd like you to act as if you have already made this decision. What is the outcome, what is different, and what do you see happening as a result of your decision?"

The moment that you can move people into the mental test-drive phase, you have given them permission to take action and they have accepted your permission. The next time you give them permission it becomes easier to accept. Remember when we talked earlier about people needing to see themselves taking some action in their mind before they can actually take it externally? Well, acting "as if" gives them that internal experience and they begin immediately to attach all of their emotions and logical justification to the process. It is also easier for them to make the decision with you because they have already done it once. They have also likely exposed any other objections or resistance that you have not yet uncovered. Once you uncover them, you simply address them and ask them to go through the "act as if" process again with their challenges answered.

In group selling we often use permission granting in a very overt yet covert way. We will simply have one person turn to another and say, "You can do this." That simple act of having the permission to do something from someone else dramatically increases the number of people who do X, for example, come to the back of the room and buy products. I will have everyone at the beginning of the program turn to one or two people around them and say, "You have permission to do whatever you need to do in order to improve your life or career today and I will support you in it."

In smaller groups simply alter the process slightly. You can get the person who can give permission to give it outright by asking that person to give his permission. I might say, for example: "Mr. Black, does everyone here have your permission to make the best and most sensible decision for the company today?" He will nearly always say yes, empowering the people in the room to make a decision. When I use this process I am regularly told that it is the first time Mr. Black has ever given his support to any project or given them the freedom to do what they need to do. Later, if the group hits an impasse, I remind them that Mr. Black gave them his permission to make the right decisions for the company. I then present them with my best solution for the company.

When groups get stuck, I use this same process to get them unstuck. I simply ask them to give one another the permission to come to the very best conclusion for the company rapidly. Or I have them give their permission to come to a conclusion within a certain period of time. By simply giving their permission, they are also agreeing to take some action within a specified period of time or to come to some conclusion that is in the best interest of the group or company.

Reassurance is the final covert way of giving permission that I will talk about here. Simply telling people that they are making the right decision and that you support their decision is a wonderful way of granting them permission. Often people want permission and reassurance simply because they fear making a poor decision. It is up to you to give your permission and reassurance so they can come to the conclusion you desire for them.

Once you have given your permission, and they have accepted it, pull back the curtain and invite them in. Show them the value again of belonging. Allow the people you have given permission to experience the delivery of all the promises you have given them. They will never be more enthusiastic than they are at that moment. From then on, you must continue to deliver an experience and a relationship that will keep them coming back for more . . . and one so powerful that if they ever leave they will constantly wonder if they made the right decision.

Permission is control—use it wisely.

Chapter Review

☛ The idea of permission is ingrained in us from a very early age. Giving permission encourages people to take the actions you want them to take.
☛ Permission gives absolution.
☛ Trials and test drives of products are covert permission grantors; use them often to your advantage.

 Success Questions

☛ In what ways can I begin granting permission in order to create change and break impasses?
☛ When should I be giving permission during my persuasion process?
☛ How can I use permission to create a cult of customers who rely on me?

 13

THE QUICK PERSUADERS

The gifts that one receives for giving are so immeasurable that it is almost an injustice to accept them."

—Rod McKuen

So far many of the major persuasion tactics have a whole chapter devoted to them. This chapter is a little different, though. It is not that it is less important, in fact, quite the opposite. These are tactics you will immediately understand and be able to apply without much practice or skill. That is also why I put them further back in the book; I want you to learn the more complicated skills first because they will take you longer to internalize.

These tactics are also the most obvious of the persuasion tactics and many people who you use them with will see them for what they are. But even if they do recognize them it does not mean that they will not work. Many times people recognize something and think they are immune. At a deeper level the process still works and has the desired effect. The Quick Persuaders are best used in a support role where you are able to group them with other, bigger tactics for an unstoppable strategy.

SOCIAL MATCHING

In his classic, *Influence—Science and Practice* (Allyn & Bacon, 2001), Dr. Robert Cialdini calls this social proof. The principle of social proof says that we determine what is correct by finding out what other people think is correct. Presenting your audience with proof or examples of what other people are doing in relation to the idea you are presenting is a very powerful way to get people to take some action when they are unsure what to do.

The reason I use the term *social matching* rather than *social proof* is that I believe that the principle goes a little deeper. I think that people have specific needs that are known to them but unfulfilled and they are constantly looking for someone else just like them. They want a social match and when they find it they will take immediate action to mimic the behavior. Simply providing that match gives you the advantage. You are doing much more than just showing them someone doing something and allowing them to have the idea that it is okay to do it too. You are carefully guiding them and telling them what they should do and then providing a match, someone else just like them who is doing it too.

In the example of social proof, the idea is that if everyone is doing something it is probably the correct thing to do. In social matching, we understand that people want to feel like individuals first but that they do not mind following along with people who are part of the "in" crowd—people just like them.

To use social matching in persuading, show as many other people like the person you are persuading as possible, but distinguish them as being special because they are similar. That simply gives people a great deal of courage to do something they might not have done before. It isn't that everyone is doing it; it is that everyone like *me* is doing it. Early adopters of products are very susceptible to social matching simply because they are in the minority and like it. They have an identity built around an idea of being first and beating the competition.

CONCURRENCE

Closely related to social matching is concurrence. Concurrence is simply an agreement in opinion. It is much easier to move the opinion of people you are persuading when you can show that someone else like them or that they respect shares their opinion.

Take the time as you prepare to persuade to find shared opinions that you have with the prospect. Start the process of persuasion with a shared opinion. Whether you share one or many opinions, it is much easier to move to a place of agreement on ideas that are new. Trust is implicit in concurrence and builds as concurrence builds.

The transference of power is enhanced when you are able to introduce an opinion that is shared by someone whom the person you are persuading trusts. It is even further enhanced when that person introduces you as sharing the same opinion.

Gathering concurrence throughout the persuasion process also makes it much easier for your audience to draw your conclusion. When persuading many, this is particularly true because of social matching, an active process that they are observing and participating in. The more people agree with you and share your opinion, the more likely they are to share your opinion on new ideas that you introduce. It also increases their likelihood of liking you, a topic we discuss in more detail shortly.

EMPATHY

Alex Mandossian, whom you will learn more about later in the book, tells a great story about the difference between empathy and sympathy. On his famous teleseminars he explains it like this: Imagine you are on a boat that is rocking and rolling in the moderate waves. Your friend standing at the rail becomes seasick, turns kind of green, and throws up over the edge of the ship. You walk over and rub his back and tell him you are sorry he is sick; that is sympathy. If you walk over to him, feel bad, and get sick and start throwing up with him because of it, that is empathy.

That is a great (albeit slightly graphic) story to make a complex idea easy. As a persuader, you want people to truly empathize with your idea. You want them to identify with and understand your situation, feelings, and motives. When people empathize with you they will rarely not find your conclusion to be the correct one.

Emotion builds empathy like nothing else. The more emotional you can make their decision, the more you can get them to relate to you and your idea, the faster they will become empathetic. By layering on experiences that others have had that are similar to their own and showing how their problems were solved, the people you are persuading become even more empathetic.

The key in using empathy is that you do not want people to feel sorry for you (sympathetic); you want them to feel *with* you (or someone else like them) to the point that they cannot imagine *not* sharing your opinion.

INCONSEQUENCE

There is a saying that a journey of a thousand miles begins with a single step. I know that quote is not about persuasion, but it easily could be.

Persuading someone fully is never the result of getting her to accept one big idea. It is a process of getting her to accept many little ideas so that the big idea is whittled down to an acceptable size. It is much easier for people to accept little ideas and small changes first. Once you have gotten them to accept one or two small ideas, it is much easier to get them to agree on the next.

Please be aware that I am not talking about the "yes set," the idea of just getting people to say yes to a bunch of things and then throwing in an idea that you want them to say yes to. That is simply a parlor trick; even if they do say yes, there is a high likelihood that they will later change their mind.

A true strategy of inconsequence is having people agree with small ideas or make small concessions in relationship to an idea that is congruent with the decision you want them to make. You will also want to attack the most influential and easiest to accept ideas first. By carefully selecting the influencing ideas you are able to slowly but surely lead your audience to a final decision that is very consequential, yet it feels like an easy decision to make.

Inconsequence is also a covert persuasion tactic because it engages the feeling of accomplishment. Once a few things have been ironed out and several agreements have been reached, it just feels good. It feels like you have momentum, that someone understands you and you understand them. It increases likeability because you now share something in common. The common bond of shared problems resolved is very powerful in deepening rapport and relationship.

Most people do not want to go over old ground. When they have solved many problems or the majority of a big problem they are open to finalizing the solution with the person they have come so far with. Consequently they are much less likely to restart the process with someone new when the promise of completion is visible on the horizon.

LIKEABILITY

Being likeable is a very valuable trait to cultivate if you hope to persuade. We all like doing business with people we like. It is much easier to accept ideas from someone we like than someone we are indifferent about.

Being likeable does not mean you have to be best friends with every person you set out to persuade; it just means you need to be pleasant and comfortable to be around. Here are a few of the traits that make us more likeable in regard to others:

- Having shared experiences
- Being from the same socioeconomic background
- Being from a similar regional area
- Having a pleasant personality
- Being well spoken and well groomed
- Refusing to gossip or share rumors
- Being knowledgeable and willing to share information
- Actively listening in conversations
- Sharing something about ourselves to further the relationship
- Using appropriate humor to add levity to situations
- Being a good conversationalist
- Having good self-esteem and generally being in a good mood

Being likeable really is not that difficult for most people. Even people who are not very likeable can be; often they are simply not aware that others do not care for their company.

Being likeable does require a constant effort, though. Each of us has our bad days or people that we do not really personally care for. If you intend to persuade the majority of the people you meet, you must be likeable to them even when they are not likeable to you. I am not suggesting you allow people to abuse you or act inappropriately. I am simply suggesting that sometimes you have to swallow your feelings and create a situation where you can get along with someone even when you normally would not.

This idea of being likeable is such a key point because it is not hard at all to turn down someone we do not care for or outright dislike. It is nearly impossible to not help those we do like if the request is reasonable. Liking is based on an emotional need. We need people to like us and we want people to like us. We are more than willing to reward those people that we like and who like us in return. Liking makes us more memorable, too. To the person who is unlikeable, the person who befriended him and liked him is memorable—just as memorable to him as the person that cut you off in traffic this morning was to you.

When choosing, we tend to choose those people we like and who are like us. In a close decision between suppliers, for example, you would be more inclined to choose the person you liked over someone you felt nothing for at all.

We like people who are like us, so be sure that you accentuate your commonalities to increase the level of mutual friendship. Be quick to lend a hand when you can. Offer advice or information that is otherwise unavailable. Find out about specific personal hobbies or passions and talk about those things. Send a note with a news article about something you discussed.

We will look more at giving to receive shortly, but I want to let you in on one of my little-known secrets right now. Every tradeshow I go to is packed with celebrities signing something. Whatever they are signing I get (sometimes two or three of them; don't be shy). It does not matter to me. Why? Because I have a cabinet full of great gifts that make me incredibly likeable.

Imagine what happens when you admit that you are a huge fan of the pro wrestler Goldberg, and a couple of days later I send you an autographed 8×10 color photo. You like me . . . probably a lot. If you look at my collection today, it contains footballs, baseballs, basketballs, minifootballs, jerseys, pictures of every size and type, books, magazines, towels, golf balls, beer bottles, makeup, and literally dozens of other things. All are signed by people from Sylvester Stallone to the San Francisco 49ers cheerleaders. And none of it cost me one thin dime. You should see all the people that think I am great now that they got such a personal gift from me.

GIVING TO RECEIVE

In addition to being liked, giving something away initiates one of our most powerfully ingrained ideals. If someone gives us something we feel obligated to give something in return. Cialdini describes this as the Law of Reciprocation. The law explains the idea; giving to receive describes the process of how it works.

Many businesses give away gifts as a means of "getting their name out there." Those gifts are often pens, magnets, shirts, mugs, or other small things that are often considered by the recipient to be throwaway items. I do not consider most of the ad specialties that cost under a couple of dollars unique enough to strongly motivate the give-to-receive action in most people. However, the more unique the gift and the more difficult it is to get, the more exclusive and desirable it becomes. When there is exclusivity and you give the gift it can have a much more powerful impact. The example I used earlier of giving away signed merchandise that I got at no charge from tradeshows is a perfect example of giving something to receive. The gift is personalized; it is specific to the person I am giving it to and there is a high desirability for the product.

While some people will respond in higher numbers to particular offers when generic gifts are sent, the numbers appear to be getting lower. For example, the free mailing labels you get from the Disabled American Veterans may encourage you to send a small donation because they gave them preemptively, but most people will either just use them or throw them away unused without a donation. The reason for the dilution of the effect is the number of people using the concept inappropriately combined with the volume of direct mail everyone receives today.

Also, a large majority of people today understand the principle of reciprocation and how well it works, so they forbid their buyers or employees from accepting gifts of any kind. Many negotiation and buying courses go so far as to explain the process and how it works and why they should actually reverse the process and give gifts to people they are buying from while not accepting gifts in return.

One of the most effective ways that you can give to receive is to give sample products or sample services for people to try out. I will often give an hour of my time to work with a salesperson who is struggling in a company that I want to do longer-term work with. That simple preemptive giving strongly encourages the desire to give me something in return. What is very interesting is that samples are expected in our society today; they do not seem like gifts and so they fly covertly under the radar of those people who accept them.

Making a concession is another way of giving to receive. It is the old idea of one hand washing the other. Making concessions early in a persuasion cycle can lead to many good returns. Know which items are sticking points that you can easily concede when you start the process and after a little bit of agonizing, make the concession. Do not make too many, though; often people, buyers in particular, will keep pushing for more and more. Ideally you will make one or two concessions in order to move the process forward knowing that you will be repaid shortly. Remember, once people get a concession, they rarely want to go back over old ground with someone else. Even if they are willing to go over the old ground, they often will not get the same concession and yours will seem more valuable to them. Give a little when it is appropriate.

ACCOUNTABILITY

One of the first lessons that was impressed on most of us was the idea of keeping our word. Being accountable is a very powerful emotion for nearly every one of us. We feel compelled to do almost everything we agree to do no matter how difficult it is for us later. Knowing the power of accountability, a good persuader gets his audience to make commitments.

Getting the person you are persuading to agree to concrete and time-oriented next steps is the very best way to initiate the drive to be accountable. In virtually every persuasive transaction I complete I will get solid next-action steps regardless of the level of commitment. Most importantly, I then follow up to let my audience know I am paying attention to the next steps and keeping track. I also try to commit myself to at least one or two next steps that I can take to show that I am accountable as well. By having some steps I can take, I also have the right to stay involved with the person in order to discuss what has occurred to date.

When I was selling for companies for a living this single idea made me the top performer everywhere I went. While other salespeople's calls went unanswered or unreturned, mine were taken with predictable regularity. The people I was calling back expected my calls, in fact in some cases nearly demanded them, because I had made a commitment to them.

When your efforts to persuade start to move in a direction you do not want them to go, you can often bring them back by pointing out the commitments that have been made. This is especially true if the person has not held up his end of the deal. Often simply bringing the conversation back in a very matter-of-fact way, something like, "We agreed I would do this and you would do that. I've completed my end of the task; is there anything keeping you from following up on your commitment that I can help you with?" The pressure to perform comes back very quickly.

The Quick Persuaders are the tools you will use every day. You will apply them in a number of situations. Use the Quick Persuaders as part of a group of persuasion tactics to support a much larger strategy and you will get better results. Think of using them like a sculptor uses a chisel, to chip away at the resistance. And like the sculptor, the last one or two blows will turn your persuasion effort into a masterpiece.

Chapter Review

☞ Quick Persuaders can be very effective but are often the most recognized attempts to influence or persuade. They are best used as part of a larger effort.

☞ Giving to receive is the most obvious of all the quick persuaders but has a very high likelihood of succeeding when the gift is very specific to the recipient. Focus your efforts.

☞ We all feel the need to follow through on commitments. Get commitments and hold the person accountable for following through. Follow through on all your commitments in order to increase the need for the other party to follow through on hers.

 Success Questions

☞ Which of the Quick Persuaders can I implement in one project I am working on today?

☞ Who should I be holding accountable that I am not?

☞ How can I get people to move into a more empathetic space with me?

14

THE PERSUASION EQUATION

Position + Presentation × Influence = Persuasion.
                                        —Dave Lakhani

This single chapter may be the most important of the whole book because it is the map for persuading from beginning to end. So many books have been written that cover all of the elements of the persuasive process and very detailed scientific models have been created that demonstrate how persuasion occurs and the processes that need to exist in order to move people or change minds. Those works are tremendously important, but the average person (you and I) does not have time to apply detailed scientific models to his or her individual situation. We need a set of tools and a blueprint for using them.

Of all of the scholarly texts that have been written to date no one has written the book that says, "Here is what you should do, and when, and this is why it works." I do not know why, but after having written this book I can guess the answer. It feels very much like you are teaching people to be manipulative. If their intention is to manipulate, this book and the principles described by other authors will definitely make them more adept at the process; again, it goes back to intent. If your intention is genuinely to help someone ethically and morally, you will be able to do that better than ever before; the same is true if you intend to get what you want at any cost. The only difference you will experience is the long-term outcome. Ultimately, manipulators are discovered, hated, and in many cases prosecuted. Excellent persuaders are revered and loved because they can move the people around them and make them experience wonder as a result.

In previous chapters I have demonstrated the most important individual tools in persuasion and given you ideas where you can use them. Now, I show you how to develop a coordinated attack using all of the skills you have learned so far together in a symbiotic way that will allow you to persuade anyone. This is the secret key to getting anything you want.

The process is very simple and includes only three steps: positioning, presenting, and influencing. In reality, it could be broken into only two steps, positioning and presenting, since influencing should be done or is done throughout the first two steps.

THREE STEPS TO EFFECTIVE PERSUASION

Positioning

The first part of the Persuasion Equation is to position yourself and your audience. Positioning consists of three elements:

1. *Persona.* Prior to beginning the process, be sure that you have properly developed your persona. Key areas to check are story, clothing, grooming, expert status, and presentation. Allow your persona to show through from the very first encounter. Before you say a word, your persona should appeal to people in a positive, authoritative way. They must recognize you for who you are—their savior, the one person who can help them solve the problem that has afflicted them.

2. *Positioning your audience.* Be sure that your audience matches your ability. Far too often the persuasion process goes wrong here because influencers choose the wrong audience for their message or they do not research and prepare their audience appropriately. It is imperative that you understand whom you are addressing if you hope to be able to use all of your newfound tools. You can influence virtually anyone, but if they do not have the power to make the decision you need for them to make, or at least to influence the person who does, then you have wasted a tremendous amount of effort.

Nearly all the unsuccessful salespeople I meet spend all of their time in this mistake. They influence and persuade the people who are easiest to influence or persuade, those people who have nothing at risk and no authority to take action. And their outcome is as expected: Nothing happens.

In positioning your audience, you need to be sure that your timing is correct and that your audience, whether one or many, is in a place where they are receptive to your message. I cannot tell you how many times I get calls from salespeople (and yes, I take all calls from salespeople just to see how well they do their jobs) whom I tell that their timing is bad and who continue to try to push their product regardless. That kind of process only accomplishes one thing—complete alienation. You want your audience to be receptive and understanding of the reason that you are spending time together. Even if your audience is hostile, the common ground you have to build on is the desire for a solution; hostile people who want a solution are positioned for one.

If you are delivering your story through a third-party delivery system, for example, public relations or advertising, be sure that your message is being directed to the right people. Sure there are people reading *High Times* who will buy your book on composting, but there are a lot more of them reading *Organic Gardening* and *Mother Earth News*. Send your message to those most likely to be persuaded and take action.

3. *Spinning your story.* Your stories should now be built in chunks or pieces so that you can customize the story to the audience, complete with specific examples and tie-ins to what is relevant and important to them. Recheck your audience and your story prior to presenting it to be sure that you have the information you need to deliver a persuasive story.

Presentation

The second part of the Persuasion Equation is to effectively present your story to your clearly defined audience. In order to present your story effectively you must accomplish two things.

In the beginning you must immediately establish relevancy and importance and develop rapport. Your presentation consists of your story and your persona, so be certain that, from the moment you appear, your persona is sending a powerful message. You want to command attention.

This is a very good time to develop familiarity. If you are speaking to a group, arrange to be introduced by a trusted member of the group who can share his or her power with you. Be sure that you write the introduction to take fullest advantage of that exchange. Ideally the person who introduces you will be very familiar with you and can talk about some personal experience he or she has had with you. If the person has had no personal experience with you, simply write in the transfer of power. I might add a line something like this in my intro that the person will read: "I know Dave is an expert on persuasion and that is why I'm so excited to have the opportunity to introduce him to you. I know you and I both will learn many new ideas. With that, help me welcome our friend, Dave Lakhani." See how carefully that is stated but how the endorsement is completely implied as well as how the power is shared. I did not say anything that was inaccurate but I did create a situation where people are listening to someone they trust introduce someone he or she trusts and respects.

If you are meeting someone for the first time and persuading one on one, this is the time to start asking questions and developing familiarity by discovering shared experiences and by getting the person to open up about himself. If you are creating advertising copy for any media, this is where you share a common problem or desire that they will have had that your product or service will solve. You enhance it with personal testimonials from others who have already experienced your solution as well.

Here is also where you quickly mentally review and adjust your stories. Your stories should be developed to utilize both the *primacy effect* and the *recency effect*. When presented with a list of information, people are more likely to remember what they heard first and last than anything in the middle. Be sure to use both effects when presenting to an individual or a group. The easiest way to remember this is the old training adage that goes, "Tell them what you are going to tell them, tell them, then tell them what you told them."

Check your story pieces and be sure they fit the group you are addressing. Add any additional information that needs to be in the story to make it complete and powerful. Practice your presentation relentlessly ahead of time so that it is polished, and can be delivered with smooth and rhythmic flow. If you are unsure how that feels, just get out a children's book and read it aloud. You will immediately get the feel for how your stories should go. There is a pace and a rhythm; be sure your story is ready.

Identify your objections and possible sticking points and address them and overcome them in your presentation. Turn challenges into opportunities and prepare to preempt your potential detractors. If there are particular issues with the physical place in which you will be persuading, correct those before you begin. Distractions break your rhythm and they allow the person you are persuading to focus attention someplace other than you.

The second thing you must accomplish in this phase is a powerful presentation. Lead with a powerful story or idea that is reinforced by a story with which your audience can identify.

Use the law of contrast to your benefit. Ask for more than you want first, and then offer what it is that you really do want. When confronted with a big decision and asked to make a smaller one, many will take action on the smaller decision.

Get your audience involved in taking action while you are persuading. Have them commit to doing small inconsequential things throughout your presentation. From setting up situations and scenarios that they can agree on, to telling pieces of your story that they can empathize with, get them on your side, get them committing to you, get them feeling for you. Make them like you and make your plights familiar and similar.

Use graphics, brochures, audio, or any other props that you need to demonstrate your point and no more. Keep as much of your audience's attention focused on you and your message as possible. This applies whether you are persuading an individual or an army.

Focus on your nonverbal language. When communicating, more than 50 percent of the cues people use to determine truthfulness and honesty come from viewing the face. Powerful persuaders videotape themselves often to see what their nonverbal communication is telling their audience.

Use good facial expression. Smile often. Smiling opens up your face, allows other expressions to flow easily, and projects confidence, happiness, and enthusiasm. Smiling also makes you approachable and human. I am 6'4" tall and weigh about 250 pounds; to some people my large chest and narrow waist is intimidating. The problem is that never once did I look in the mirror and feel intimidated. When I first started speaking about persuasion, I was so passionate about the topic that I forgot to smile when I talked and people felt I was aloof, unapproachable, and aggressive—not at all the outcome that I wanted. By simply reminding myself to smile at least once every minute, I was able to completely turn my audiences' perceptions around and now crowds of enthused people come up and visit with me after my talks.

The people you are persuading are not mind readers and some of them are not very good at picking up the subtle hints you leave behind, so you must ask them to do something or tell them what you want them to do next. Present your request in a way that is consistent with their expectations and that is consistent with your presentation: Project confidence and expectancy of compliance when you ask.

Install a reticular activator. A reticular activator is a device that allows you to describe what people will literally see or experience after talking to you that will remind them of your conversation or presentation. With a reticular activator, you are simply tying pieces into your story that will remind people and pull them back into the ideas and emotion of your story at a later date. They also reinforce what you said about a particular event. An example of a reticular activator for someone who is a fund-raiser for Special Olympics might be, "Each time you see someone in a wheelchair from now on, you have to ask yourself: 'What can I do right now to help someone in challenging circumstances achieve exceptional opportunities?'"

Future pace what you want them to do and experience. When you have people in a peak emotional state, in person or in writing, have them move forward in time and experience what their life, their emotions, their existence will be like after having been doing whatever you are suggesting for a certain period of time. Or have them imagine the emotion they will feel from having made a good decision or having helped. A great question to ask while you persuade is, "Looking back at the decision you made today five years (or any appropriate time frame) from now, what will be different and how will you feel because of the decision you are making right now?" One of two things will happen. They will see the result of either not making the decision or of making the decision; each gives you the opportunity you need. If they have made the decision and they are happy then you are well on your way. If they have not made the decision you get to find out what they believe will happen if they do not and show them how to avoid their self-described inevitability.

If you are persuading a large group and want to individually persuade after the talk, then you want to draw a large group of people to you after you speak. Tell a very engaging and emotional story and stop just before you finish the story. Tell them your time has come to an end so anyone who wants to hear the rest of the story should see you at the back of the room. This works exceptionally well with voice mail as well. You simply begin the story and say, "I'm afraid I'm running out of time; call me back at this number and I'll finish the story when you find yourself intensely interested."

Influence

Influencing your audience is the final step in the persuasion equation. Applying every individual tool you have studied in the preceding chapters as often as possible is the key to enhancing your influence. Careful application of the tools will build your position to one of overwhelming advantage and swing the tide in your favor. Elements of the final step of the persuasion process are really included in every previous step. Throughout your interactions with the audience you are persuading, you must apply all of the appropriate influencing principles every step of the way to build tremendous power and opportunity to persuade.

Initiate the principle of giving to receive wherever you can. Giving people insider information (ethically and legally, of course) can work well. Giving them access to your Rolodex or access to your network in some creative way is also very effective. If you can give the audience you intend to influence something first, use the opportunity. Interestingly, the cost of the item does not have to be high (though the implied price and value can be very high), simply relevant to your audience, to be effective.

Use transference whenever possible, whether implied or active. Recruit or meet people who already have influence and authority over the people you hope to persuade and get them to endorse you in some way, either explicitly by having them endorse you in person or in writing, or implicitly by being seen with them, being photographed with them, or quoting them in your presentation.

Build on your audience's beliefs and their desire to believe. Reinforce current or long-held beliefs; tie your own beliefs together with theirs. Refocusing their beliefs and getting them to be active in creating new beliefs that involve you gives you the advantage, particularly when it comes to bigger efforts of persuasion like building a brand.

Reinforce your authority or expert status in appropriate interactions and in a way that benefits those you would like to influence most. This is the time to layer on the personal testimonials, the articles that you have written, as well as examples of the media that have covered you. This is where you also want to make very conclusive statements about what needs to be done. You need to be sure and definitive in your presentation, providing answers to questions and proposed solutions. There is no room for weakness or lack of certainty here. If you are uncertain, create a break so that you can quickly gather the information you need.

Cause your audience to be curious and to engage you in more detailed conversation and questions. Pose scenarios, difficult questions, or surprising opinions. Show them ways that non-conventional thinking has created breakthroughs or solutions and get them actively participating in creating new ways of thinking by asking better and more detailed questions. Challenge their answers and ask questions that require them to become more and more specific in their responses. Lead them to the conclusions that you have already come to and to the conclusions that you want them to arrive at through your questions.

Use availability to reinforce why taking action now is imperative. As I was writing this I got an e-mail announcement from a business associate who is selling a high-end training program for $1,497. The e-mail told me he had only made 700 copies of the program and each was individually serial-numbered and once all 700 were sold he would make no more, period. About four hours later I received another e-mail that let me know he had already sold 392 copies of the program and time was running short to get my copy; he also let me know that even if I ordered now and mine was order number 701, he would have to refund my money. I have to admit, because of the second e-mail, I had to take a long look at the web site and what he was selling just to be sure I was not missing out on something that I would later regret. That is an excellent example of limiting availability and increasing desire with time pressure.

Another way of effectively using availability is to increase the pressure of time as in the example above. Time can be measured in many ways, but ultimately it always comes down to you needing to do something in order to get some benefit quickly or it becomes unavailable or more expensive—that is the reason coupons have expiration dates. Time can also be limited in relationship to a project: If a decision is not made by a certain time there will not be enough time to get the project started or completed within the specified time frame. Costs can also be increased with time as well: You get a better deal for buying now than you do if you wait, or you are given incentives that will not be available later.

Use the concept of inconsequence to get people to take little actions that lead to bigger actions. When my mom joined the cult, they did not ask her to give up her life savings, become totally subservient to men, and abandon her friends. They simply invited her to dinner to meet some people. That couldn't hurt. Those people invited her to a service—that couldn't hurt. The minister invited her back. That did not seem like too much of a commitment, so she went. At the next service, the minister invited her to the altar to accept Jesus Christ as her personal Savior. That was a lot bigger step, but logical in the progression of things. And one small step led to another. You can do the same things with your clients. Getting them to agree to a series of next steps that you will take together is inconsequential. Then, deliver on your end of the deal by getting your steps done as quickly as possible and report back. Hold them accountable by asking them to take the steps they agreed to. When they know you will be doing your part and following up to be sure they have done theirs, they become more likely to follow through because if you are familiar and liked, they do not want to let you down.

Accountability is closely tied to inconsequence because people are more willing to be accountable for small outcomes than large ones.

By now you can see the importance of layering on the different tools in order to create higher levels of persuasion. At this point, your persuasion process may have lasted a few minutes or days depending on your desired outcome and the layers of persuasion needed. In future chapters we overlay the persuasion equation on the selling process, creating powerful advertising, writing persuasive copy and letters, and the negotiation process. Step by step, we position our stories and our audiences, present our message powerfully to our carefully identified audience, and layer on persuasive tactic after persuasive tactic to methodically break down natural resistance, to increase the emotions of acceptance and desire, and finally to move the decision to the outcome we have chosen.

Be aware that the Persuasion Equation can be applied in person, in writing, on the Web, on television and radio, or in just about any area you have the opportunity to influence another person.

While manipulation is far less complicated, it is predatory and its impact is fleeting. The Persuasion Equation may seem complex at first, but it really is not. With just a little practice it will became a part of who you are and how you operate just like eating or breathing. It will become a skill that you are unconsciously competent at using and you will be consciously aware of its results. The Persuasion Equation is universally applicable and gives you the opportunity to persuade with unbelievable efficiency; it is a skill that will set you apart and serve you well for the rest of your life.

 Chapter Review

☛ Remember the equation: Position + Presentation × Influence = Persuasion.

☛ Clearly define the message that you are going to send as well as your desired outcome.

☛ Clearly identify your audience before you present.

☛ Layer the elements of persuasion as appropriate throughout your message to intensify the impact.

☛ Practice the Persuasion Equation until it becomes a part of who you are and until you apply it in every situation without even thinking. This ability is the essence of the professional persuader.

(Continued)

Success Questions

☞ What current situations could be enhanced by applying the Persuasion Equation?

☞ Which audiences am I wasting my time with and whom should I be talking to instead?

☞ As I evaluate my current opportunities, which of the elements of persuasion should I layer into my current process?

☞ Whom do I know who follows this process well and how can I get involved in having him or her mentor me through the process?

☞ Looking back over deals I have lost, what could I have done differently in order to persuade them to come my way?

 15

PERSUASIVE SELLING

Everyone lives by selling something.
—Robert Louis Stevenson

To some it will seem odd that in a book on persuasion there is a whole separate chapter on selling. But persuasion, as you have learned, is much more than simple presentation of features and benefits and hoping someone will accept your argument. Persuasive selling is rather the careful development of an environment where the person who will buy your product can make only one good and logical decision.

I demonstrate a very straightforward sales process here that virtually anyone can remember and apply successfully. I also explain how to make it more effective using many of the different tactics you have learned so far. I want you to remember that no matter what you are trying to persuade someone of, you are selling. All of life is sales. There are no exceptions.

I have discovered over years of teaching people to sell and

managing sales teams that the problem of selling is broken down
into one of these four areas:

1. You do not like to sell.
2. You do not understand selling.
3. You do not like salespeople and your salespeople know it.
4. You are not selling the way the prospect wants to buy.

The old saying that people do not like to be sold to is true.
But everyone loves to be given all of the information needed
to make a good decision; wouldn't you agree? Ultimately, that
is what selling is: giving people enough compelling information to make a completely informed and obvious decision.
Closing a sale is nothing more than simply bringing the decision process to a logical conclusion. Notice that nowhere did I
say pressure them, sharp-angle close them, negotiate, or anything else you may have learned or heard about how selling
works.

Here is the hard truth about your business. If you are going
to own or grow a business you had better get comfortable with
selling, and fast, because all business is selling at some level. That
does not mean that you have to personally enjoy going out to
find and close the business yourself. But you had better understand what it takes and how to measure how well it is being done
in your business, and you had better respect those people who
are doing the job you dislike, if you decide to hire salespeople
and delegate that task to them.

It is imperative that you learn something about selling if
you hope to make your marketing work. You have to know
what the process is to get people to spend their hard-earned
dollars with you. They *are* going to spend their money and it is

up to *you* to understand what is required to get them to spend it with you.

If you do not have time to go through this process fully or if you are so involved in either running the business or delivering the product or service then you need to hire someone who can sell for you. When you hire someone to sell for you, you must pick someone with a documented track record of success, who has significant sales experience and/or documented sales training and preferably industry or product-specific experience that can be brought to bear immediately on the customers frequenting your business. You then need to be positively sure the people you picked understand how to persuade. The best thing you can do is give them this book to read in their first week (great sales-people have likely already read it) and if they haven't had traditional sales training, get them involved in a program so they can learn a complete technical methodology.

When we teach sales training we teach a complete process that begins with gathering leads, and ends at serving the customer after the sale. Here is the interesting part: We do not teach that process until the end of the training so they can overlay the persuasion techniques at every step. We require marketing departments to be a part of the training as well when we do the training for companies in-house. Far too many businesses allow a partial and often complete disconnect between sales and marketing and this is an enormous mistake as both are deeply involved in persuading customers.

Rather than giving you the full sales seminar here, I would like to give you a short course on how people buy so you can address clients in the way they would like to be addressed in order to get them to do business with you. I also demonstrate different persuasion tactics you can apply throughout the process.

WHAT YOUR CLIENTS WANT

There are certain things your clients desire:

☞ To be made aware that they have a need or to have their need validated

☞ A relevant solution

☞ Answers to their questions

☞ Detailed information to make a good decision

☞ To be reassured they are getting what they need and are making the best decision (value)

☞ For you to give them permission to make the decision right now

There really is no secret to selling; if you can provide all of this, you will get the sale every time. People simply want to be served. By being relevant, answering their questions, and demonstrating value, you not only set their buying criteria, you heavily weight it in your favor.

Selling really is that simple. The harder you make it, the longer it takes for you to get the aforementioned information to them, and the longer the sales cycle. I use an acronym, "I SELL," to make understanding persuasive selling easy to remember and apply. The I SELL process looks like this:

I—Identify qualified prospects.

S—Start your story.

E—Educate, answer, and encourage.

L—Lead them to their best decision.

L—Let them buy.

Identify Qualified Prospects

The first step to persuasive selling remains: Be relevant. You must first identify those people who have a need and are a good fit for your product or service. The biggest mistake I see both beginning and experienced salespeople make is wasting time with anyone who will talk to them. If you cannot qualify prospects as being a good fit for you before you start talking to them, you had better be able to do it in less than three minutes or you will waste huge amounts of your profitable time.

One of the oldest tricks in the sales manager's arsenal is helping salespeople figure out the value of their time. Most salespeople will never take the time to do it and, if they do, will lack the dedication to apply it on a daily basis. On the other hand, there is a top 5 percent of salespeople who will live and die by that number on a daily basis because they know how much money they need to make and how much time they have left in which to make it. Let me ask you this question to see if I can drive home how important this one idea is. If you had 30 days to make $10,000 to save the life of someone you love, would you go fishing with your buddies every other day? Of course not; you would be intensely focused on your goal until you got there.

If you have never done this exercise before, I want you to do it right now. Simply write down the amount of money you want to make next year. Divide that by 2,080, the number of hours you work in a typical year. That will give you the value of each one of your working hours. Divide that by 10-minute segments and then you will know precisely how much money you are willing to invest in someone before you move on. Let us say you want to earn $100,000 per year, the bare minimum for a great persuader. The equation looks like this: $100,000 divided by 2,080 = $48.07 per hour divided by 6 (10-minute segments) = $8.01.

For every 10 minutes you spend on anything you are investing $8.01. Every activity you do has a price and none is higher than the amount of time you will spend with an unqualified person and here is why. Because for every hour you spend on unqualified people or time-wasting tasks you have to subtract it from the number of hours you have left to earn your $100,000 or you have to add back in extra hours (nights, weekends, holidays, and vacations) in order to make up for the ones you threw away. When you do the math and are honest about the amount of time you waste you will realize the value of speaking only with qualified prospects.

Be sure that you are quickly and efficiently qualifying your clients. Questions you must ask are:

☛ Does this person have an immediate need I can solve?
☛ Is this person working on an intermediate-range project on which I can help?
☛ Does this person have the authority to make the decision, or does he or she honestly have influence over the project with the person who does?
☛ Will I be able to interact with the ultimate decision maker at some point prior to the decision process?
☛ Is the person or company financially able to do business with me? (Do not judge a book by its cover—you must find out factually.)
☛ Do all of the required technical conditions exist for the person to use my product or service?

☞ Does this person have the requisite experience to use my product or service?

☞ Are there any other conditions that cannot be met that would disqualify this person today?

Start Your Story

Once you have qualified the prospects, it is time to start your story. Before you start the story be sure your audience understand they have been heard. Make sure they are ready to listen when you start. A prepared audience is an audience preconditioned to buy.

You should already be in persona and ready to tell your story in person or over the phone; but if you are not, make any necessary shifts that are required to have your full-blown persuasive persona out front for inspection by your prospects. If you are on the phone, your voice should be clear and crisp. Here is another tip from Susan Berkley, CEO of The Great Voice Company: Do not clear your throat on the phone; have a sip of water instead. No one wants to hear you clear your throat. If you are in person, be sure that your attire is impeccable and that your voice, posture, and presentation are fully prepared.

Start your story by reiterating the important issues the prospective client brought up. Show you heard what she had to say and then launch into your story. If you have crafted your story well, it will include many persuasive elements and chances to ask more clarifying questions.

During the story it is important to use the principle of transfer of power. Be sure to use case studies or testimonials to reinforce what you are saying. Be sure the testimonials and case studies are relevant to the issues the prospective client has.

Educate, Answer, and Encourage

As you tell the story, build insatiable curiosity. Make your prospects have to ask you questions that take them deeper into the story as a result. As your story educates them, answering their identified questions, you will educate them about specifically why you and your solution are best for them. You will have built plenty of credibility and demonstrated your experience through the proper use of transference of power and credibility. But they will now have more questions.

You now have the opportunity to take them even deeper because you know that the more time you can get them to invest with you, the less time they will spend with your competition. Through the process of educating, answering, and encouraging, you prompt them to give you more and more pieces of information that you use to layer on the persuasion and set their buying criteria. The more you educate them, the more you become their guru or expert and they understand that they can rely on you. The more they rely on you the less likely they are to rely on anyone else.

Quality of information wins this portion of the process as well. The best-thought-out and best-reinforced answers that are relevant will turn the tide in your favor. Be sure that your answers are tied together with exactly how your solution will solve their specific problems. Encourage them to challenge or question your solution, so you can get to the root of their real concerns at this point. Continue to educate, answer, and encourage until they have all the information they need or have requested.

Lead Them to Their Best Decision

This is where your money is earned. As you continue telling your story, you begin to get your audience to make small decisions and agree to things with little consequence. You are conditioning them for the ultimate decision.

The more small decisions you can get prospective clients to commit to at this stage, the easier their decision to do business with you at the end. If you are selling cars, you might get them to acknowledge which color they like or what accessories they will want in the car. If you are selling technology, it might be getting them to agree on which locations would be their test sites and identifying which people would be involved in the process. By actively getting them to take these small actions in their minds, you move them into a place where they must see you and your product involved, since you are standing right in front of them answering their questions.

During this phase you also clear the stage for the final decision of either making the purchase or taking next steps. If all questions are answered and the prospects are ready to buy you move right into the next step—let them buy. Many sales cannot be closed in one day. But in order to be in control of the persuasion process, you must stay in control of what happens next. So during this phase you clearly determine what the next steps will be. You get them to agree to dates and timelines for the next steps. You also clearly identify who is responsible for what at this stage to be sure that you are initiating the tactic of accountability. People will most often do what they promise when they know someone else is going to be holding them accountable.

If the decision to buy at this point has not been reached, it is imperative that you are vigilant about meeting your agreed-upon deadlines and commitments. The prospects will be judging you by your ability to perform. They will also be giving you a number of clues as to what kind of a client they will be over time. Pay particular attention. Do they meet their deadlines? Are they able to meet their commitments? Are they relying on someone else and if so, why? Every piece of information you can gather at this point is crucial to your long-term success. Again, the persuader with the most information controls the process and wins. Continue recommitting the prospects as necessary and meeting goals and deadlines. This is a great time to give to receive. Provide the company with specific information that is immediately beneficial to them, do favors where possible and ethical, and do the same with specific gifts or giveaway items that can tie your prospects to you. Again, make sure all efforts at giving to receive are ethical, legal, and allowed by both your company and theirs.

Continue this process until it is time to make a decision. You may need to direct them to the decision earlier than they are ready to make it and the way to do that is through the use of exclusivity and scarcity. You can use scarcity by demonstrating how lack of a decision will affect their timeline or delivery schedule. You can also demonstrate it with manufacturing backlogs or other client placement that moves them lower down the fulfillment chain. Fears of loss or delay in deliverables are powerful motivators in the persuasion process. Demonstrate exclusivity to add another layer of desire. Show them how they will become part of a group or receive special incentives available only to early adopters or people who buy within an identified period of time. Demonstrate how their decision will give them access to a special group of people or events they would otherwise be excluded from.

Let Them Buy

The final step of the I SELL process is to let them buy. I cannot tell you how many times I have watched salespeople talk themselves out of closed sales. At this point they feel a need to keep talking and keep persuading and reassuring to the point that it causes confusion or hesitation. When your prospects are ready to buy, *sell*.

They will have at this point convinced themselves they are making absolutely the right decision. Get them deeply involved in the process of the mechanics of buying right away. If that means drawing up a contract, then get it done immediately and get them started on some project that will have them taking the first steps of implementation. If it means simply taking cash, then get them to the point of sale. Once you have begun the process, it is perfectly acceptable to up-sell. If you are selling retail, offer your higher-margin add-on products now. If you are selling high-ticket items, this is the time to up-sell warranties, insurance, or whatever else it is that you can to increase the size and profitability of the transaction. There is no better time to ask people to buy something else than when they are actively involved in buying.

Once you have sold to customers the very first time, you move them into your ongoing influence cycle where you will develop the relationship and their loyalty while creating multiple opportunities for them to buy more from you more often.

When you start thinking of selling in the proper context it really is a lot of fun and you begin to realize that selling is really the part of your business that gives your customers the most and best information they can get. Selling is where people are served—the rest is delivery. What you do after the sale is the extension of that first experience that continually reminds them of the great decision they made. It also reminds them how easy and smart future purchases will be. They will not have to ever pay attention to another ad again because they will never be better served than they are already by you.

Remember, selling is nothing more than stacking the appropriate sales tactics onto one another to support your story for a predictable outcome. The I SELL process is the easiest way I know to guarantee the persuasive selling success.

 Chapter Review

☞ Remember the acronym I SELL—Identify qualified prospects; Start your story; Educate, answer, and encourage; Lead them to their best decision; Let them buy.
☞ Layer on appropriate persuasion tactics along the way.
☞ Be sure to generate curiosity and create desire continually throughout your story.
☞ Let them buy. When they have made their decision, stop talking and start facilitating.

 Success Questions

☞ Do I adequately qualify the people I sell to today?
☞ How much money do I waste on unqualified prospects per year?
☞ Have I committed the I SELL process to memory?

16

PERSUASIVE ADVERTISING

Let's say you have $1,000,000 tied up in your little company and suddenly your advertising isn't working and sales are going down. And everything depends on it. Your future depends on it, your family's future depends on it, other people's families depend on it. . . . Now, what do you want from me? Fine writing? Or do you want to see the goddamned sales curve stop moving down and start moving up?

—Rosser Reeves, *Reality in Advertising*

The next paragraph will make a lot of people mad and it should. It should also make them think and help you earn more money. If it does nothing else, it will let you make an informed decision the very next time you create an ad.

Far too few people understand what makes adverting persuasive today and far too few business owners know how to understand if it is profitable. Most of the people writing copy and creating ads do not have a clue what makes ads work. I am not talking about the people who work in big agencies, though many of them do not understand it either. I am primarily talking about

171

the people who create your ads. They are the guy at the newspaper or trade magazine who throws your ad together, or the on-air talent on your radio who writes ads when she's not on the air and voices them, too. They are also the frustrated directors who work at large ad agencies or small cable stations. It is the lady down in marketing who used to be the receptionist but over time was promoted to the marketing manager's position, and the technical writer who you promoted to be your copywriter because . . . well, he can write. These are the people who create advertising that rarely works and it is your fault—you hired them.

Now that you are hopping mad, let me tell you there is hope. None of those people have bad intentions. Quite the opposite, in fact. They want you to make money, so let us show them how. In this chapter I show you a great formula for creating advertising that works. There are two steps to making your advertising persuasive and profitable:

HOW TO CREATE PROFITABLE AND PERSUASIVE ADS

1. Create ads that interrupt and tell a persuasive story.
2. Measure them.

Rather than giving you a whole class on how to write the perfect ad or a long list of words that sell better than others, I will do something even better. I will give you the most carefully adhered to and most powerful copywriting principles you will ever learn so you can apply them to the ads you are creating today. I will show you how to get the information you must have to make your ads effective. These principles apply to print, radio, television, Internet, signs, banners, direct mail, and even your on-hold messages. If you take these principles to heart and apply them to your ads and your marketing model you will be able to dominate your market faster, better, and at a lower cost than your competition.

Before I go any further I want to talk to you in more detail about why it is not a good idea to have your ads created by your ad representative or their team. Think of the sheer volume of ads that these people are responsible for creating on a daily basis. They are responsible for creating hundreds of ads a year, many of them for your competitors.

Here is how it goes when the ad rep gets your ad. Either the ad rep or a copywriter in the office asks you for a few important points you want to get across. Almost always those points are all about how good you are, your service, your hours, your convenient location. They also want you to throw in some special sale price that will help drive business. Then they go to work writing your ad.

Put yourself in their place. Imagine if you were faced with writing a dozen ads a day for a multitude of businesses, some of whom are your competitors, some that require a great deal of thought and some that should but are not going to get it. What would happen? Sure, you would think hard for a few moments, then you would start thinking about all the other ads you wrote and pull the best phrases and ideas and offers out and put them together in an ad . . . *your* ad. Is that what you *really* want?

The result of this approach is predictable and typically not at all persuasive. What happens instead is that your ad sounds or looks just like your competitor's ad, which causes one of two things. Either it gets lost in the rest of the messages it is competing with or it will *reinforce* your competitor's message if they have higher-frequency and more consistent advertising than you.

Along those same lines goes the idea of copying the ads that your competitors are creating or being all the places they are because that must be what works for them. The reality is that if you copy your competitor's ads you only help reinforce their message. The most important thing you can do in an ad is to find your own message and drive it home. You have to tell a story that only you can tell. The chances of your real competitors knowing what the right thing is to do with their advertising are very slim and copying them is not a good idea when it comes to the message you are sending. The other problem with copying is that if their advertising is working and you do not have the budget that they do or the same goals it can still be counterproductive.

I want you to try this exercise quickly to see what I mean and to see how easily you can make your ads better and more engaging. Look at your current ads through a different filter, just for today. Suspend your beliefs about what is good or bad about your current ads and simply apply these principles to your ads, and you will see how powerful they become. If you agree that your ads can change for the better then you are on your way to increased business. If you cannot make your ads better, then congratulations; you have got one step of the process out of the way . . . or you are dangerously close to losing a tremendous amount of business.

Here is what I want you to do: Get out your print ads, your TV ads, your web site, your direct-mail letters, your yellow-pages ad, and your radio ads. Get them arranged so that you can work with them for just a few minutes.

Now I want you to replace any reference to yourself or your company with your competitor's name or logo and ask yourself this question: Would anyone know the difference between us if we switched logos or names? Also ask yourself, Can my competitors say the same thing about themselves that I do about myself?

Are you a little surprised by your answer? If in any category most people can say basically the same thing accurately and factually, how hard does it become for a potential client to make a buying decision? Why would they choose you over your competition based on the information you have just given them?

Do you give up? So did your valued prospect. They settle for the first person who answers the phone, or their question, or who has the lowest price.

Now do you see why competition is so brutal in your category and why you have reduced yourself to competing on price? On the other hand, can you also see how easy it can be to set yourself apart and compete on value instead of price?

Before I give you the components of a good ad, I want you to keep some of the advice of Rosser Reeves, one of the nation's best advertisers ever, in mind: "You must make the *product* interesting, not just make the ad different. And *that's* what too many of the copywriters in the U.S. today don't yet understand" (*Reality in Advertising*, Knopf, 1961).

The operative word in that quote was the *product*: People do not want to hear all about you and how great you are and how great your business is and how lucky they are to do business with your exceptional employees. They want to know that the product you have will do what they need and that you will be able to help them be sure they have all the information they need to make a good buying decision. If they are first convinced of that, then come into your store and have the experience they expect, then and only then will they begin to believe your stories of quality, service, and employee superiority.

Discovery, uncovery, the reality of you, are all different ways of saying the same thing. If you want to know what is different about you, what makes people want to buy from you (or *will* make them want to buy from you), you have to dig in deep and find out what it is. You have to ask very detailed questions about your business, your products, your customers, your history, and yourself. Only after you have dug through all of that will you come up with your own uniqueness or your unique selling proposition—that one thing your whole story can be built around.

Let me give you an example. I have a client called Fidogear (www.fidogear.com). They make dog collars, coats, booties, leashes, and harnesses. Not all that remarkable, is it . . . or is it?

What if I told you Fidogear was founded by a 70-year-old grandmother who loved dogs and wanted not only to do something in her retirement to stay busy, but also to help dogs? What if I told you every single item they sold with the Fidogear label was made by hand and it was made specifically for your dog from measurements you send in? Now what if I told you their products were priced the same as the ones you find at the local superstore? Are we are getting somewhere, particularly as we build layer upon layer of why you would want their products if you value your pet? Uniqueness is what makes you who you are and what makes people come to you in a world of sameness.

Here are some of the questions I want to ask you to find out what is unique about you:

☛ Tell me your story: How did you get started in this business and why this business?
☛ What are you passionate about in the business?
☛ What does this business do for you personally?
☛ Why have you chosen the products that you have?

☞ What would people be shocked to know if they knew this about your business?

☞ What do your competitors try to copy of yours?

☞ What do you do for your customers that consistently, pleasantly surprises them?

☞ Why do you do it?

☞ What problems are you solving for your customers?

☞ What frustrations do prospects usually have when they are shopping for your product or service?

☞ How do you add value to your products or services that your competition does not or cannot?

☞ How do you know?

☞ When was the last time you shopped your competition?

☞ Tell us about your background: Why are you an expert in your business?

☞ If you are not an expert in your business, what would you have to do to become an expert?

☞ If you could only tell a prospect three things about your business and they would make a buying decision based on those three things, what would they be and how would they be different than what your competitors will say about themselves?

☞ Why specifically would they be making a good decision based on those three criteria?

☞ What do people have to hear every time before they will buy from you?

☞ What are the three most common questions you get when people are trying to decide to buy?

☞ Who is your number-one competitor and why?

☞ What is it that you know about your product or service that you wish people could just understand? Why is that important?

By doing very detailed discovery with yourself and your employees you get one level of information. Next you do the same thing with a select group of clients, those people who are buying from you consistently . . . your good clients. In addition to the appropriate questions we just discussed I want you to ask them these questions:

☞ You are a great customer of ours and we want to attract more people like you. What makes us your first choice for X (insert your product or service here)?

☞ What do we do better than anyone else in our category?

☞ Why is that important to you?

☞ Could you imagine doing business anywhere else? If yes, tell me about that. If no, tell me why.

☞ Can you tell me the process that you went through in order to choose us?

☞ What do we do consistently that surprises you?

☞ What is unique about you that makes us a good fit for you?

☞ What could we do to make your experience here the best and most memorable experience you have ever had in this situation?

Now you have added another layer of enlightening information from which you will create your most persuasive ad ever, but we will go one step deeper just to be sure we have gotten all the information we need. We will go to a good customer who has quit using you or buying from you, and ask these questions:

☞ What made you switch from us?

☞ What could we have done to serve you better?

☞ What is unique about you that we were not serving that made you switch away?

☞ Is there anything that could ever make you come back and be a client again?

☞ Can you tell me the process by which you chose your current supplier?

☞ Was there anything we did that you wish your new supplier would do?

☞ How long did it take to make the decision to change from us to a new supplier?

☞ Is there anything that is not happening with your new provider that they could do that would make you happier?

☞ What would make you switch away from this supplier to someone other than us?

With that final layer of complexity and answers to those questions, you end up with a tremendous pool of information from which you can pull some very surprising and powerful ideas, information, and stories that will be the basis for your uniqueness and for your ads, the kind of ads that grab people's attention. As a bonus, you also find a lot of information that you can use to improve your service.

CREATE ADS THAT INTERRUPT AND TELL A PERSUASIVE STORY

So what are the qualities of a great ad? The most important thing to remember about any ad (or any persuasive message) is that you are simply telling a story designed to gently interrupt, compel, persuade, and have the audience take some action.

All great ads have a headline no matter what the medium.

The purpose of a headline is to interrupt, grab attention, and sell you on the very next sentence or idea. It must be something that hooks you and pulls you in. The goal of a great headline is to interrupt the general malaise that overtakes us when we experience ads on television, on radio, or in newspapers and magazines. The headline grabs us by the ears and speaks directly to us about what is important to us or it grabs us by the eyeballs and forces us to read it, which compels us to read the next sentence.

Persuasive ads focus on me, not on you. To earn my attention, you have to let me know what is in this for me. If your ad cannot immediately set you apart from the competition in a way that makes me ask why I am not considering you, it is not going to work. Great ads speak directly to the person you are persuading; they create a one-on-one conversation that tells a story, answers questions, and compels us to learn more or take action.

Nearly all great ads ask a question relevant to me and then answer it. They include documented evidence of success, reliability, experience, and so on, and do not rely on unsubstantiated fluff statements like "Ours is better than the competition." If you want them to believe you, transfer the power and credibility of someone I trust or someone who is like me to yourself so that I can trust you too.

Exceptional ads give clients a real reason to believe what you are saying is true. They use third-party endorsements and testimonials to do their proving for them. No one wants to be the first one to dip a toe in your water; they want to know others already dipped their toes in and pulled back a golden slipper, not a stump.

Highly persuasive ads use words that allow us to create dynamic, beautiful pictures in our mind that include us in them. They speak to us on different levels. They get us involved sensing, seeing, hearing, and feeling. If you want to really bring up memories that people have, ask them to remember what something smells like. When I ask you to think of new-car smell, which car do you think of? If I ask you what it smelled like in your grandmother's house, I bet it takes you back. If I tell you that not properly drying your carpets after cleaning them will leave them smelling like a baby's dirty diaper, I bet you get a whole different picture. But do you see how easily a sense like smell pulls you in and causes you to have an experience?

Perfect ads not only set up the criteria by which every competitor will be judged but create a standard that only *you* can meet. Great ads set you apart from your competition. When you can put their name or logo in place of yours and say there is no way they can say this about themselves, then you have got an ad that has a real chance of being successful.

It is imperative that your ads make use of words, images, and phrases that put me in the picture, that demonstrate something I can understand that has happened or that I am afraid will happen to me if I do not use this product or service. Great ads are clear, succinct, and free of jargon or trendy words that many people may not understand. They must also have a binding quality— something that ties all these ideas together congruently. It will also tie it to your mind so that you know what you are hearing or seeing and who it is. This is where branding begins to occur over a long period of time.

Another quality great ads have is a single focus that is driven home over and over again through any medium where the prospect may experience it and is not changed until a new campaign is started. You must always remember the purpose of advertising is to sell something to one person at a time.

Finally, great ads focus on one idea or action item per ad. If you have 10 things to say you say it in 10 separate ads. Be sure every ad has a call to action that tells your prospects what to do next.

It is imperative you spend time focused on writing, rewriting, and researching your ads to get them perfect. But writing and rewriting is not enough; you must be able to determine their effectiveness in creating new customers and new revenue. If they are not doing either, then you must discard them and try again. If the bar is not moving higher your ads are not working.

I want to leave you with a few last tips for creating good ads: Be sure that your ads have a rhythm, like a song or a poem, that they have a beat, a feel that compels you and takes you on the ride with them, that encourages you to continue and keep the pace. Many times I find that when I am writing ads it helps to listen to music as it reminds me of pace and rhythm. In visual media the words create the rhythm for the visuals and the visuals are harmonized with the message to create a powerful outcome. I encourage you to look at a lot of ads to begin to find that rhythm and feel and see how you can incorporate it when you create your own ads.

If you have never written an ad before, here are a couple of books that will help you get started and that will also help you better evaluate ads that others write for you:

David Ogilvy, *Ogilvy on Advertising* (New York: Crown, 1983)
Dennis Higgins, *The Art of Writing Advertising* (New York: McGraw-Hill, 2003)
David Morrell, *Lessons from a Lifetime of Writing* (Cincinnati, OH: Writers Digest Books, 2003)

Here is a good concept for you to keep in mind. Great ads can be created inexpensively and expensive ads are not always great. Unless you are a professional graphic artist or production person, get some professional help to have your ads look and sound their very best. The only award you need to worry about your ads winning is the six-inch Ben Franklin award, the one that fits nicely in your wallet or bank account.

If you are not coming up with the answers you need or ads that work, make the investment to hire someone who can create the kind of ads that will work. You will easily recover any amount of money you invest in ad development through ads that pull better and bring in more paying customers than ever before.

MEASURE YOUR AD'S EFFECTIVENESS

The ultimate measure of how well your ads are working is how much more business you have this year over last. But there are other benchmarks you can and should use as well. When measuring dollars, you should measure every day, week, month, and year. By measuring in this method you can predict trends, and know when your advertising is effective and when something is not working. It also gives you feedback you can use to make your ads even more persuasive.

Traffic to your store or calls to your business are good indicators of how responsive people are to your message. Keeping track of traffic counts year over year is a very simple way of determining what is happening when you start a new campaign.

Documenting an increase in sales of a particular item or service being advertised is an effective way of determining ad effectiveness. If you intend to focus ads on the sale of one product or service it must be either a large enough sale that the campaign remains profitable or you must have add-on sales that make the overall sale large enough to justify the campaign.

If you increase the effectiveness of your marketing many times you will see close ratios increase dramatically. This happens for a couple of reasons: People are reminded that they wanted to buy your product or service and finally take action, or those people who are on the fence are moved to action because you gave them new or compelling information that caused them to take action.

Using specific toll-free numbers or telephone numbers to track an ad, particular landing pages on your web site, or special offers segmented by media can be effective in helping you better determine how effective your advertising is in a particular media. This is a lot harder to do with a small budget but can be done. You simply present a series of ads on radio, for example, and then evaluate what happens over the period that they run. Then move your ads to another medium and test again. There are inherent problems in this kind of test. One medium may be very effective at targeting instant buyers while another has more impact with buyers over time. Another problem is how well targeted one medium was over the other. However, if you are testing an impulse or instant purchase this can be an effective means of measuring. If you are going to use a testing methodology like this over the long term, you need to test a campaign over at least one quarter before you move to another medium and test there.

Asking is probably the most common form of tracking and the least accurate for a number of reasons. First, most people do not remember where they heard about you first, if at all. That accounts for all the people who told you they heard about you on television when you have never been on television. People try to be helpful, so they guess. If you are going to ask you have to ask for specific information: What station did you see me on, Which yellow pages do you use, What radio station do you listen to? Asking is somewhat more effective with print where you can put an identifier in the ad that you can ask them about that would indicate which ad generated the response.

The most important thing to remember about tracking is to do it. Tracking is one of the most critical components of making your business grow and for creating more persuasive ads. There is no substitute for good information to help you make better decisions. If you are not tracking, start today and you will be instantly more profitable as a result.

Through this chapter you learned not only how to make your ads more persuasive, but how to quantify whether they are working. By simply taking the time to review the results of the effort you expend you will be able to make your ads more persuasive and put a monetary value on the messages you are sending.

 Chapter Review

☞ Persuasive ads are stories well told with a moral that involves the audience taking some action.

☞ Persuasive ads tell me one thing at a time. They do not try to cram too much into one exposure. They make a point and drive it home.

☞ Persuasive ads make use of nearly all of the persuasion tactics you have learned throughout this book.

(Continued)

Success Questions

☞ What can I say conclusively about my business that none of my competitors can say of theirs?

☞ Who is my audience and what is the story I most want to tell them?

☞ In reviewing my old ads, what can I see that should be done differently in future ads to make them much more effective?

☞ Are the right people creating the messages I want our company to send?

 17

PERSUASIVE NEGOTIATING

*In business, you don't get what you deserve, you get what you
negotiate.*

—Chester L. Karrass

For many businesspeople, negotiation is one of the hardest and most misunderstood tasks they will ever be called on to do. Just the simple thought of the word *negotiation* for many brings on one fear: that they might lose. Negotiation when done appropriately should leave no one a loser. Everyone should feel as if their needs were met or that the right thing was done. In my experience the only negotiations that were not pleasant were those where one side either rightly or wrongly felt the other was taking advantage of them.

Often when negotiating people fall victim to their prejudices and rather than making well-founded decisions they begin to make irrationally emotional decisions. Many times those decisions are based on irrational beliefs or even hidden beliefs that most people do not believe they have.

There is a great tool on the Internet at www.implicit.harvard .edu that allows you to test your prejudices about a number of things including race, sexual orientation, weight, disabilities, and many more. It is very interesting to see what you consciously versus subconsciously believe about some things. It is often our unconscious prejudices that keep us from achieving what we want. We do not even see the roadblocks to our success because they are buried within.

In order to be a persuasive negotiator you must have congruence within yourself. You must also maintain a very clear idea of what an appropriate and acceptable outcome should be. Far too often, people start their negotiation process with unrealistic or unachievable goals. When that happens no amount of persuasion will result in a successful negotiation. In fact, quite the opposite will happen; more conflict will arise, and parties will become more emotional. Finally, everyone is left in a position where they have to defend their unreasonable position and no one can win.

Describing negotiation as win-win is the politically correct way of discussing what outcomes should be. Reality on the other hand is quite different. Everyone who sits down at the negotiating table has one goal in mind, to get the best deal possible for himself or herself. With that in mind, it is important for the superior persuader to understand that he or she can attach *no* emotion to other people's outcome. One can only focus on creating an outcome that allows the other person to feel at the conclusion of the negotiation that the outcome is exactly as desired, or at least, acceptable. Victory truly does come when both parties' needs are met, but in some cases, one person will walk away feeling like a winner and the other like she did not get what she wanted. What has to happen when other people walk away not getting what they wanted, is for them to understand and agree with the reason for the conclusion. If they do not, often they will break the agreement and the process has to start again or move to a different level. When thinking of negotiation, I think Robert Estabrook summed it up when he said: "He who has learned to disagree without being disagreeable has discovered the most valuable secret of a diplomat."

Virtually all of the tactics of persuasion that you learned earlier in the book apply here. The overriding consideration you have to keep in mind when you are hoping to get someone to give you some concession is, "What do I have to offer in this deal?" If you have nothing to offer, it is not a negotiation at all; it is simply a job of selling and you need to take that approach. Negotiation by definition requires give and take. You have to know what you stand to lose and what you are willing to give up in order to protect it. Many times for professional persuaders the end of a selling situation requires some negotiation. Often it is terms or margin or even the commission the salesperson earns that will be on the table.

To begin the negotiation process persuasively, you must enter the process from a position of power and authority. That means being fully informed. You must know hard-and-fast facts about what can and cannot happen. You must know which items are flexible and which are immutable. You must also know which ones can be traded off, for example, longer warranties for payment up front. Once you know what your boundaries are, you need to do a little research on the boundaries of the person across the table from you.

One of the things I suggest you do early if you know that a negotiation is imminent is to talk to other suppliers or people who have negotiated with the person or company in the past.

See if you can find out what his style is, find out how flexible he is, and find out what concessions he has made. By doing that you begin to get a feel for how you can present your case and what to expect in return. The more prepared you are at this stage, the less bluffing can occur.

Openness and honesty are critical keys to developing rapport and trust when the process is opened. You must insure that your persona matches not only that of the person that you are working with but that of the person you will be negotiating with. If, for example, you have been working with a corporate real estate manager up until the point of the negotiation and for the purpose of the negotiation you will be speaking with her attorney, adjust your persona. Be sure that your clothing is on the same level as hers; be sure that you are prepared ahead of time with a list of ideas and expectations that you are ready to discuss.

Negotiations should only be undertaken by two people who have the authority to agree on decisions at the table. If you are not meeting a decision maker it is to your significant advantage to wait until you can. Not letting a decision maker come to the table to make agreements is a stall tactic.

When you begin negotiating always lay out your most desirable outcome first. You need to ask specifically for what you want. Many times simply by setting the expectation early the person you are persuading will accept that as the outcome he needs to work to and will work toward that end. If you start low, it is very difficult to raise the stakes later and it gives you no room to make concessions. Part of effectively persuading during a negotiation is the give to receive. If you can make a concession first, it makes it much more likely (and easy) for the other person to make a concession of his own. If you are paying careful attention, you can use your concession to get him to give a bigger concession to show that he is in fact the more benevolent person.

If you have set yourself up as an expert appropriately, many times that stature can be carried into the negotiating room with you. This is especially important when you are negotiating with someone whom you did not convince in the first place. If you will be negotiating with someone other than the person you convinced, it is nearly always desirable to have the person in the room. The reason is very simple. He has made a commitment to you and he is going to be hard pressed to break it. He also has a very big stake in the outcome because he is emotionally committed to having what you have agreed upon. It also takes away a lot of the fakes and feints that other professionals negotiating the deal may try to throw in. If there was an agreement on a specific issue, questions about the agreement can be settled by asking the person who made it.

Negotiation is also a patient game of questioning. The more information you can gather from the person with whom you are negotiating about her personal outcomes as well as her personal beliefs about the process, the more likely you will be to present an agreeable outcome.

Whenever possible, link likeability and familiarity to influence the person you are negotiating with. Get them to talk off topic about issues even as simple as the weather. Agreement that it is a beautiful or horrible day outside gives you something in common, a shared reality that you can build from. It seems very simplistic, but remember how the cultists work. They start with a core belief that most people have, an idea of a savior and salvation, something you can both agree on. From there it is simply a matter of building on your shared beliefs.

There are seven steps in the process of negotiation that you will want to follow to be most persuasive:

1. Whenever possible, let the party with whom you are negotiating present her proposal first. Often you will find that she is offering more acceptable terms than you were willing to accept. The negotiation is finished before it starts. If she is not, it gives you the opportunity to see what her position is before you reveal yours. You have the opportunity to adjust your pitch before you give it.

2. Test assumptions to see what is truly negotiable and what is not. If someone says "We always do X," question it. Ask if there has ever been a case where they have not done it or where they would not do it. Try to find out if it is a hard-and-fast unbendable rule or something that could be different. Acknowledgment that something could be different means it is not an absolute.

3. Once you have tested something, let it rest a little. Put it on the back burner and propose that you want to address other issues first; get some agreement on inconsequential things. Come to agreement on the things that you know you can agree on first. The more you can get other parties used to agreeing the more chance you have of finding a good solution that will work for all of you.

4. Do not respond to emotional issues. In nearly every negotiation someone will try to play "hardball." Simply recognize it for what it is and continue the process. If he keeps pushing, address the issue and his behavior directly. Experts and authorities have nothing to prove; address people's behavior and be willing to walk away if they are unreasonable. Understand that in every negotiation there is the possibility that one of you will not agree and will walk. Do not be afraid to be that person in the appropriate circumstance; it can give you power later.

5. Lay your cards on the table. Before you can come to agreement about what you will or will not do, everyone needs to lay their cards on the table. Often this will break an impasse. If I understand you cannot meet my terms because it will bankrupt you, it would not make sense to have you start the project. We simply have to find another way.

6. Close the negotiation by reiterating what each party will do and documenting next steps. Once that is done, follow through on the steps. Be sure to get reassurance that everyone understands the negotiated outcome.

7. Finally, to seal the agreement, continue to persuade. When possible, have dinner or send some gift to the person or people with whom you negotiated. First, by initiating the idea of giving to receive, you have given them something and expect in return they will maintain their level of commitment. Second, it reinforces the idea that you are in a partnership and have mutual trust and concern for one another. Obviously this is not something you can always do, particularly where the negotiation stems from a set of negative circumstances. But even then, you can acknowledge others in some meaningful way, even if that acknowledgment is to say you are sorry that things got to this level but that you appreciate them for coming to agreement. This is not a time to be prideful; it is a time to ensure that your agreement sticks.

Keep in mind throughout, like all persuasive situations, the most flexible person will persuade best. Be sure that you develop rapport at some level and maintain it. Stay focused on the big picture but pay attention to the small details. Keep score and use it only when necessary. If you have made a lot of concessions, point them out and make it known that you have given plenty and now you need something in return.

When the negotiation comes to a successful conclusion be happy. Negotiations can be a great deal of fun; they are much like a chess game with all players doing their best for themselves. Once concluded, review what else you could have done to be more persuasive because this time will not be the last for you. And, the more you know, the better you will be the next time around.

 Chapter Review

☞ There can be winners and losers in a negotiation and both parties can still move forward.

☞ All of the persuasion tactics you have learned throughout the book should be applied during the negotiation.

☞ You must continue to persuade after the negotiation to be sure the agreement sticks.

☞ If you reach an impasse or strongly emotional period, allow for a cooling off period; give calmer heads a chance to prevail, and give yourself some time to regroup.

Success Questions

☞ Do I have to win in every negotiation encounter in order to achieve my goals? If so, can I acknowledge and be happy with the wins that I have had even if I do not achieve my ideal outcome?

☞ Can I remain emotionless throughout the negotiation even if the other party does not?

☞ Do I have the courage to walk away from the table if my needs cannot be met?

☞ Do I always make sure I am negotiating with the decision maker or with the decision maker present?

18

PERSUADING THE MASSES ELECTRONICALLY

When I took office, only high energy physicists had ever heard of what is called the World Wide Web. . . . Now even my cat has its own page.

—President Bill Clinton

I f you are to persuade effectively, you must learn to persuade electronically. In this case, I am not talking about electronic broadcast media like radio and television; rather I am talking about how you persuade using Internet technologies.

While many people have spoken about how to use the Internet, very few people have truly explored how you use the Internet to persuade. Fortunately many of the same rules of traditional media apply, but there are some significant and noticeable differences of which you should be aware.

I want to say one thing conclusively: Using the Internet to persuade your audience, whether an audience of one or one million, is mandatory today. The Internet is a predominant force in all of our lives. It gives us nearly instant access to information that might have taken us days or even weeks to find in the past.

That access makes it imperative that you are capable of persuading via the outlet people will turn to in order to verify the information you have given them or to find you in the first place.

There are several technologies the best persuaders use on their web sites to convey their messages. The first technology is the web site itself. Your web site needs to present an image that is congruent with your persona and the image of your company. I cannot tell you how many really impressive people I meet who look great, sound great, and have a powerful message. Then, I go to their web site to find more detailed information and the site looks like it was designed by a rank amateur with no graphic design, writing, or persuasive ability. My first reaction to the person suddenly becomes incongruent with my reaction to the web site. I have to then immediately question whether the person is as successful and knowledgeable as he had first appeared. People do judge you by your web site.

I am neither a web site designer nor a graphic artist, but I do know a few things about what makes web sites persuasive. First, the site must be quick loading and easy to navigate. I should be able to find any information I want on the site within two or three clicks. Second, the site must be graphically pleasing. It should be laid out in a way that is conducive to reading. That means no wild blinking lights, funky fonts, or layouts that do not flow easily. Third, the site should have enough information to answer my questions and give me a way to easily reach you if I have more. It will also have a newsletter or other regular communication vehicle from you so that I can hear from you and develop a relationship. That should be set up using an autoresponder so anyone can sign up instantly and receive your information. It also helps you build a list of people who enjoy your work—people who become ideal persuasion candidates. Ideally you will have your contact phone number prominently displayed on every page of the site. Fourth, the site will incorporate both audio and video in important areas. The great advantage of the Internet is that it allows people to have the communication experience they want the way they want it. They can read, listen, or watch at their convenience based on their personal tastes.

Audio and video will be two of your most powerful weapons in your campaign to persuade online. During my research for this book I had the opportunity to visit with Armand Morin, founder of The Big Seminar, unquestionably the best electronic persuasion seminar in the nation today. He is also a co-founder, with Alex Mandossian and Rick Raddatz, of Audio Generator and Instant Video Generator. Armand told me how simply adding audio to his site in one key area improved persuasive responsiveness by over 300 percent. According to Armand, specifically telling people what to do audibly when they get to your site greatly increases the effectiveness of the site. In the example of increasing persuasive responsiveness by 300 percent, Armand simply had a small audio file that automatically played when anyone clicked on the web site. The file said, "Before you go any further, fill in the box to the right with your name and primary e-mail address so we can send you a valuable report about X." This demonstrates the power of the idea that people want to know what to do, but they do not want to spend a lot of time figuring it out.

Web pages should also have headlines like any other ad. The headline should tell me what information I can expect to find below it and why that information is important to me. Or, it should ask me a very compelling question that will force me to dig deeper for the answer. Keep your web sites interesting and informative. People still consider the Web an informational tool first and a commerce tool second. If your site does a good job of providing information and persuading, you will have a winner.

Closely related to web sites are blogs. Blogs are web logs that are able to be edited very easily by a user. Anyone who can use a word processor can write a blog. The best analogy is to think of a blog as a daily journal. A blog is a daily or weekly journal of your latest thoughts or ideas on a specific subject.

By the time you read this you will have probably at least heard of a blog, if not read one, because of all the attention they received during the 2004 presidential election and the Iraq War. Blogs are powerful for several reasons, not the least of which is the fact they are ranked higher in most major search engines than many web pages because of the relevance of key words and the current nature of the content. I have a blog I use for my consulting practice (you can read it at www.boldapproach.com— simply go there and click on the logo) that has me ranked much higher than my most significant competitors for key words like *advertising* and *marketing*. Without that feature, I might have to pay $5 to $10 per click in a pay-per-click search engine like Google to get a similar ranking.

Blogs are also powerful because they give you an outlet for your ideas and a place where people can read and comment on them. Because blogs are beginning to be seen as a viable media outlet, the media are increasingly searching blogs for information and experts they can interview about every topic under the sun. Using a technology known as RSS, or real simple syndication, people can subscribe to your blog and have it sent right to their desktop every time you post something new (or at whatever intervals they desire) so they can have your most current thoughts when you share them. Each of these web technologies does two things: It creates a following of people who like you and it gives them exclusive access to you in some way.

HOW TO PERSUADE THE MASSES FOR THE COST OF A PHONE CALL

Teleseminars or teletraining is the simplest way to persuade a group of people "in person" without having to travel to see them. Teleseminars are different from a traditional conference call in that they are filled with people who have been attracted to you through your books, newsletter, web site, blog, or some other medium. They have a desire to hear what you have to say. They are your followers and they want access to you.

Alex Mandossian is the nation's foremost expert on teleseminars and earns a seven-figure income every year through teleseminars. He also developed a unique persuasion tool called the Ask Database. I spoke with Alex and he generously shared the most important issues around persuading people via the phone or via teleseminars. Not surprisingly, Alex uses many of the techniques you have learned in the persuasion tactics chapters of this book but with a few unique twists.

Alex says that to communicate via a teleseminar effectively and to persuade people to take some action, you have to speak in pictures. You must get people involved in the action for them to remain interested. It may seem that keeping people's attention on the phone for 60 to 90 minutes would be difficult because they cannot see you and you cannot see them so multitasking or drifting off is very easy to do. Alex uses a twist on an old idea: He gives his participants cheat sheets to fill out while he leads the class. According to Alex, "I want your attention focused on me. If I keep you writing and taking notes, you have to stay with me. The more actively involved I can keep you, the higher the likelihood of your taking the action I want you to take."

Using metaphor and active verbs pulls your audience in on the phone or in person, so be sure you are using picture words and action words to describe what you want your audience to do. The more involved you can get them in the picture, the more persuaded they will be at the end of the day.

Be sure to lead your call with a strong hook that gets people's attention right away. On most 60-minute conference calls the largest number of listeners will be on the call during the first 20 minutes. If you are selling something you want them to buy at the end of the call, you want to have your first call to action at the end of that first 20 minutes. Does that format sound a little familiar? It does if you have ever watched an infomercial. About a third of the way through the infomercial there will be a call to action. You should then give another solid 20 minutes of content, allow a little time for questions, and spend the last 10 minutes of the call making your most persuasive case for taking action and buying now.

If you are using teleconferences simply to educate an audience as part of an ongoing sales process, you should stay focused on content for the full duration of the call. I personally like to give a chance for questions about 20 minutes into the call and again about 40 minutes into the call. Questions are very powerful because if one person asks, many are wondering and you have the opportunity to serve the group well with your response.

You should record every one of your teleseminars. Once you have recorded them, you can then add them to the library of information on your web site. You can also turn them into audio books or special reports that you give away as gifts to those people you hope to influence. If you give them as a gift, be sure they have a monetary value associated with them. Most business-related audio books today cost at least $24.95; yours should too. Remember that people still consider the Web a source of information. The more information you can provide for your potential clients, the more likely they are to ultimately be persuaded by you. The more they read and study information from you, the more they become believers and followers.

HAVE YOUR OWN RADIO SHOW

There used to be only two ways to have your own radio show. The first was to get a degree in broadcasting and get a job on the air if you could. The second way was to buy time on the air and create your own show. Option number two is still very viable and a good consideration if you hope to persuade large groups of people to your way of thinking. You can get on the air in many areas of the country for under $100 per hour per week. That is a very small investment to build an audience of people who agree with you.

There is a new way to create your own radio show called *podcasting*. The advent of digital music devices has led to this revolutionary idea. The idea is that virtually anyone with about $200 of recording equipment and a personal computer can create a radio show. Done correctly, the show has an intro and music that leads into you talking. The show is set up just like a regular talk program you would hear on broadcast radio but, rather than being aired, it is podcast, that is, sent to an aggregator who collects podcast programming and sends it directly to your audience's e-mail inboxes. Former MTV VJ Adam Curry was involved in creating the very first podcasting software and aggregation site on the Internet, called www.ipodder.org. Like a blog, people simply search for programming they want to hear, subscribe (typically at no charge), and get new feeds from you as often as you create them.

Podcasting is a great way to deeply persuade a narrow niche audience. I have used podcasting effectively to reach traveling salespeople and business owners. Many successful salespeople and business owners end up in their cars or on planes with great regularity. As a result, many own digital music devices and would much rather learn than simply listen to music. I set my podcast up in a traditional radio format and even include "commercials" where I promote my products or myself. Not only am I persuading them and setting myself up as an expert, I am also selling my products and service to a willing audience who has requested to hear me. Radio is very random in terms of who will hear you when. Podcasting on the other hand is very targeted because your listeners were typically searching out very specific information when they found you. For a complete overview of podcasting and how to use it to sell, visit the web site www.howtopodcastforprofit.com.

It is important you keep abreast of all the current technology available that will help you persuade. I am creating a web site to support this book so I can keep you up to date on all of the latest persuasion technology developments at www.howtopersuade.com. Be sure to stop by often and learn about everything available to help you be more persuasive.

Chapter Review

☞ You must have an effective web site if you intend to persuade on an ongoing basis. People need some way of finding out more about you.

☞ You should include audio and video on your web site to make it most persuasive.

☞ There are many tools like blogs and podcasting that not only enhance your expert status, but also help you identify those people who like you most and are easiest to persuade.

☞ Teleseminars are the most cost effective way to persuade the masses without seeing them in person or leaving your office.

 Success Questions

☞ What technology can I immediately use to persuade my audiences more effectively?

☞ What changes do I need to make to my current web page to make it congruent with my persona and my business image?

☞ What changes do I need to make to my web page to make it easier to use and more informative?

 19

MASTERING PERSUASION— THE ART OF GETTING WHAT YOU WANT

You must train your intuition—you must trust the small voice inside you which tells you exactly what to say, what to decide.
—Ingrid Bergman

Persuasion, like any other skill, is one that is mastered through practice and application. It is imperative if you hope to persuade at the highest levels that you never stop learning. In order to master persuasion you must keep careful notes of those situations that worked exceptionally well and those that were notable failures. You must deconstruct and analyze each to find the clues to your success. That deep analysis is what trains your conscious thinking so that you can decide exactly what tactic to apply and when. More importantly, it trains your subconscious mind and helps train your intuition. It is that part of you that is interpreting the world around you and giving you subtle hints, warnings, or affirmations about what you are doing.

Persuasion truly is the art of getting what you want. Most of us throughout our lives have failed to reach the levels of success that we dreamed of, and not because it was not available to us. We have failed to reach those reasonable goals because we have failed to persuade those who can help us achieve them. And the biggest reason they will not help is because we have not asked them. People cannot help you achieve your dreams of success if they do not know they exist. But remember, as Zig Ziglar says, "You can get everything in life you want if you will just help enough other people get what they want" (*Secrets of Closing the Sale*, Berkley Publishing, 1985). The art of persuasion is identifying what the people you are persuading want and helping them achieve it.

The art of persuasion has served me very well over the years. What started out as an obsession with understanding how something went so wrong turned into an understanding of what makes everything work out right. Interestingly I have found that persuading myself is no different from persuading someone else. There is a part of me that has to get something out of whatever it is that I am convincing myself to do: If I am satisfied with the outcome, my thoughts become congruent with my actions and I have persuaded myself. If not, I continue to repeat the same behavior I hoped to eliminate or change. Sometimes I simply act "as if" to see if I could reasonably adopt a new behavior. I would ask you to act as if you were an excellent persuader even if you are not sure it is what you want to do. Try it for a week and see what it means to you. Often you will find it is not as difficult as you think.

I want to leave you with six tenets that will make your efforts to persuade extremely effective every time. Think of these as a part of the framework around which your persuasive efforts are built.

SIX TENETS OF PERSUASION

1. *Outcome Based.* In order to persuade effectively, your goal for the person being persuaded must be clearly defined. You must effectively present your goal in a way that allows the person being influenced to make the best and only obvious decision. You will continually define, clarify, lead, and allow the person to draw *your* conclusion.

2. *Best-Interest Focused.* The best interests of the person or the group are paramount and always considered as part of the influence process. Persuasion simply does not work long term when it is focused on serving only you. You must have the best interests of those you will persuade in mind. If you do not keep those interests in mind, your ability to persuade any group of people will be fleeting. There is also great potential for harm both to you and the people you persuade if your intent is to manipulate rather than persuade.

Remember the example that I gave you earlier of my experience in a cult. At the end of the day, the group still has a large membership, although many of their methods had to change in order to continue to recruit. The majority of the people I was personally involved with simply left. Many of them went on to have significant problems in life including addiction, suicide, and repetitive failures in their personal lives. That is truly the outcome of manipulation. The people most responsible for the manipulation and deceit in the group that I belonged to are now facing the same issues. They lost all credibility; no one would believe them. They could not keep up the façade forever. The result is that not only was their manipulation exposed, they lost their own identities.

3. *Truthful.* Persuasion professionals tell the truth. While spinning events to better suit their message is perfectly acceptable, they do not intentionally mislead or lie in order to create their outcome. There is no room in professional persuasion for dishonesty. The old idea that at the end of your day you will be known for something is never more true than here. Professional persuaders will either be known as the people others want to be around and work with . . . or they will be known as confidence tricksters, shady operators, and liars. Choose well before you choose to persuade.

4. *Goal and Time Oriented.* Influencers have specific goals and time frames set to reach milestones. If they cannot influence a certain person or group within a specified time frame related to their goal, they simply move on. Time is too valuable to waste on people who will not come to your way of thinking when appropriate.

Often I hear salespeople tell me that the economy or a war or any other number of problems kept them from reaching their sales quotas. To that I say *hogwash*. At any given time someone is buying what you are selling. People will always buy what they want. I am not suggesting that selling and persuading people to buy will not be difficult sometimes, but it is not impossible. The only reason that people do not make a quota or convince someone is because they are not focused on the investment of their time, or their product or service is no good. If your product is no good or you do not believe in it yourself, immediately stop trying to convince other people it is right for them. You can never be congruent. Instead, use your highly developed persuasion skills to get the job of your dreams. If I am going to sell in a tough environment, I spend a great deal more time carefully identifying my prospects so that I can maximize my effort with each of them.

5. *Personal.* Influencers get to know the people they intend to influence; they do not simply pick targets of opportunity. Manipulators pick targets of opportunity because they can afford to burn through people; you cannot.

The most valuable clients you will ever have are those who have already purchased something from you and who feel they were well-served. They help you spread your gospel, they bring their friends and neighbors to you, and they happily give you their endorsements.

It is okay to have two sets of friends—those who are very close to you and those you cultivate simply for the purpose of gaining business. Do not feel like you cannot categorize people; you can, and there is nothing wrong with it. There are many people whom I consider casual friends that I know a lot about, that I socialize with on occasion, who are only my friends because of what we can do for each other. We still have to persuade each other regularly, but it is much easier to persuade them than someone I have no relationship with at all. I have a complete set of friends that is much smaller and much older that I would do anything for with no expectation of anything in return. There is no need to persuade these friends—they would do anything just because it needed to be done. Can you see the difference? Once you do, you will become a much more effective persuader.

6. *Ethical.* If you want to persuade professionally or simply effectively you must remain focused on ethically moving people in a positive direction for the best good of all involved. There are no good reasons for forgoing ethics. Through the early part of this decade we have seen what happens when people and companies lose focus on their ethics. It is not just the individuals who

are harmed. It is the thousands they touch. In today's easy-to-reach society, one slip in ethics can harm hundreds, if not thousands, of people.

IMMEDIATE NEXT STEPS TO PERSUASION MASTERY

This book will serve as a solid foundation and reference to which you can refer in specific situations or often as a refresher. When you are able, come to an in-person training. You will learn so much more interacting with a group of people from different walks of life, cultures, and experience. You also get to see nuances of persuasion that no book can cover. I want to give you a gift for buying my book and for spending this time with me. I would like you to have a monthly newsletter. Please go to www.howtopersuade.com and sign up. There you will find out about the latest discoveries, ideas, and thinking as it relates to persuasion. Since you own this book, the newsletter is my gift to you.

At the end of this book you will find a list of resources and a bibliography. I strongly recommend all of the books in the bibliography. Wiley, my publisher, is one of the largest and best publishers of persuasion material today. You will be well-served by visiting their web site (www.wiley.com) as well and discovering what is available. On the web site www.howtopersuade.com, you will find a much more detailed list of resources and reference material. I encourage you to visit often as I will be updating the web site with not only those resources but also recorded interviews and other learning opportunities. If you will let me, I would like to be your personal mentor as you begin to persuade better and more effectively every day. Practice and application are your keys to mastery.

I look forward to your success as you persuade more effectively each day and I look forward to hearing your stories. Take the time to drop me a note or anecdote about what you have learned and accomplished after reading this book. I would love to post your story on the web site for others to learn from as well.

Remember, everything you are involved in requires some level of persuasion. You now have all the skills you will ever need for getting what you want. Go out and persuade someone to help you get it. Your biggest reward may be in your next conversation!

PERSUASION RESOURCES

Throughout the book I have referenced several people or outlets to learn more about specific elements of persuasion. I wanted to open my Rolodex of the world's best in the most important aspects of image consulting, teleconferencing, the Internet, and purchased radio.

At the web site www.howtopersuade.com you will find a host of other resources that you can use including information on Instant Audio Generator, Instant Video Generator, and the Ask Database, and where to buy radio time to host your own radio program.

CLOTHING

Steve Reeder
Tom James, Inc.
www.tomjames.com
208-938-5245

Tom James specializes in custom and ready-made clothing that will fit any budget. Steve Reeder is by far the most knowledgeable person you can talk to. Tom James comes to your location to fit you and is available almost anywhere nationwide.

GIFTS

Jon Clark
Clark and Christopher
www.palmtreepromos.com
941-235-0271

Jon is the foremost expert on corporate gifts and customized merchandise that you can give your clients. Jon's advice on the topic is regularly seen nationwide.

IMAGE CONSULTANTS

Mercedes Alfaro
First Impression Management, Inc.
www.firstimpressionmanagement.com
888-324-6243

Mercedes Alfaro is the president of First Impression Management, Inc., and a specialist in executive etiquette and professional image management.

Maggie McQuown
Visible Edge Inc.
www.visibleedge.com
972-247-0234

Maggie McQuown specializes in dressing you for persuasive success.

Judith Rasband
Conselle, Inc.
www.conselle.com
801-224-1207

Judith is the developer of the Style Scale, in my opinion one of the best tools to use to get dressed for any occasion.

INTERNET PERSUASION

Armand Morin
The Big Seminar
www.bigseminar.com
919-570-3409

Armand is the nation's foremost expert and trainer on Internet persuasion. His Big Seminar has trained thousands of people on critical elements of successful Internet persuasion.

TELESEMINARS

Alex Mandossian
www.askmylist.com
415-382-1212

Alex Mandossian trains the nation's best teleseminar presenters. If you want to persuade by phone you want to talk to Alex.

Shannon Seek
Seek Solutions
www.rentabridge.com
866-924-8856

Everything technical you need to do a teleseminar. The best tele-
conference line provider in the nation.

VOICE COACHING AND TRAINING

Susan Berkley
The Great Voice Company Inc.
www.greatvoice.com
800-333-8108

Learn from America's top voice coach and trainer; I have never
spoken to anyone better.

RECOMMENDED READINGS

PERSUASION

Joseph Campbell, *The Power of Myth*, 2nd ed. (New York: Anchor Books, 1991).

Robert Cialdini, *Influence—The Psychology of Persuasion*, 2nd ed. (New York: Perennial Currents, 1998).

Robert Greene, *The 48 Laws of Power* (New York: Penguin Putnam, 2000).

Robert Greene, *The Art of Seduction* (New York: Penguin Books, reprint edition, 2003).

Kevin Hogan, *The Psychology of Persuasion* (Gretna, LA: Pelican Publishing, 1996).

Robert Levine, *The Power of Persuasion* (Hoboken, NJ: Wiley, 2003).

Kathleen Kelley Reardon, *Persuasion in Practice* (Thousand Oaks, CA: Sage Publications, 1991).

SALES AND MARKETING

Jeffery Gitomer, *The Sales Bible*, 2nd ed. (Hoboken, NJ: Wiley, 2003).

John Klymshyn, *Move the Sale Forward* (Aberdeen, WA: Silver Lake Publishing, 2003).

Dave Lakhani, *Making Marketing Work* (Audio Book) (Boise, ID: BA Books, 2004).

Jay Conrad Levinson, *Guerrilla Marketing*, 3rd ed. (Boston: Houghton Mifflin, 1998).

Blaine Parker, *Million Dollar Mortgage Radio* (Philadelphia: Xlibris, 2004).

Annette Simmons, *The Story Factor* (New York: Perseus Books Group, 2002).

Jon Spoolstra, *Marketing Outrageously* (Bard Press, 2001).

Mark Stevens, *Your Marketing Sucks* (New York: Crown Business, 2003).

Elmer Wheeler, *Tested Sentences That Sell* (Upper Saddle River, NJ: Prentice Hall, 1983).

Roy H. Williams, *Secret Formulas of the Wizard of Ads* (Bard Press, 1999).

INDEX

VALUABLE FREE GIFT
FOR BUYING THIS BOOK

I want to make this the most valuable book you've ever purchased, so I'd like to invite you to one of my powerful $1,495.00 persuasion events held around the country each year as my VIP guest so I can train you personally.

Simply sign up at www.howtopersuade.com and bring your copy of the book to the event, and you get in FREE! Plus, I'll sign your copy of the book showing that you've been personally trained to persuade by me.

If you'd like to bring your whole team, simply buy each of them a book and give it to them right now. At each event I'll also have surprise special guests who will teach you other methods of persuading online, on the phone, and through your persona, as well as many of the other aspects of the areas covered in the book. This is an event you won't want to miss. Your book in hand is your free pass; anyone without the book will be required to pay $1,495.00 to attend.

I look forward to meeting you and to exploring persuasion with you.